A Call to the Church
from Wang Ming-dao

A Call to the Church
from Wang Ming-dao

呼籲眾教會

王明道

Translated by: Theodore Choy
Edited by: Leona F. Choy

CHRISTIAN LITERATURE CRUSADE
Fort Washington, Pennsylvania 19034

CHRISTIAN LITERATURE CRUSADE
Fort Washington, Pennsylvania 19034

CANADA
Box 189, Elgin, Ontario KOG 1EO

GREAT BRITAIN
The Dean, Alresford, Hampshire

AUSTRALIA
P. O. Box 91, Pennant Hills, N.S.W. 2120

NEW ZEALAND
512 Dominion Road, Auckland 3

Copyright © 1983
Leona F. Choy

First Edition July 1983
ISBN 87508-094-4

All Rights Reserved. No part of this publication may be translated, reproduced, or transmitted in any form or by any means, electronic or mechanical, including photocopy, recording, or any information storage and retrieval system, without permission in writing from the publisher.

PRINTED IN THE UNITED STATES OF AMERICA

Contents

	Wang Ming-dao—The Man & His Writings	7
1.	Nitty-gritty Faithfulness	15
2.	Obey God or Men?	23
3.	Preparation for Suffering	29
4.	The Missing Voice	35
5.	Look at God's Servant	45
6.	Success & Embroidered Pillows	51
7.	A Young Opportunist	59
8.	A Message Without Discount	65
9.	What to Expect from the World	71
10.	Touchstone of Obedience	77
11.	A Plot that Boomeranged	83
12.	Determination	89
13.	Strange Men & Amazing Miracles	97
14.	The Echoes of Life	105
15.	Two Suicides	113
16.	Why Fear Threats?	121
17.	Why Hang On to Life?	129
18.	When Christ Stands Up	135
19.	Relaxing Your Vigilance	141
20.	An Imported Prophet Fails	147

王明道

Wang Ming-dao

The Man—Iron Turned to Steel

WANG MING-DAO—crusader, prisoner, servant of God. He referred to himself as a trumpet sounding a call for righteousness. What Christian patriarch was this whom the Communist government of China felt necessary to silence for twenty-three years?

Born to the Wang family in 1900 in Peking (now Beijing), China, he was given the name Tie-zi, meaning "iron." Not until he was twenty and considering Christian ministry did he adopt his now famous name, Ming-dao, meaning "revealing or understanding the Word." Affected by the intense strain of the bloody Boxer Uprising, his father, who worked in a Methodist hospital in Peking, committed suicide before his son was born. After a stormy and unsettled boyhood in extreme poverty and a corrupt environment, Wang became a Christian at the age of fourteen.

Immediately he accepted for himself the high standard of God and His Word, and the foundation was laid for the high moral discipline that characterized his life. Even in the revolutionary heat of accusations and "struggles" against him prior to his imprisonment, no attack on his personal character could succeed.

Wang could not decide whether to become a politician or a preacher, his speaking and writing abilities suiting him for both. With Abraham Lincoln as his hero, he drove himself in academic and spiritual discipline. When he surrendered his political ambitions, he was baptized with some of his zealous young friends in a frozen river in the dead of winter as a symbol of his determination to follow Christ fully.

When the anti-foreign issue was rocking the Chinese churches during the Japanese occupation of China, Wang Ming-dao and his church stood apart because his church had no foreign origin or missionary connections. He avoided any patronage from the West and consistently refused to go abroad for theological study or even to accept preaching invitations overseas, shunning both as temptations to pride. His was a true Chinese Christian expression of the "three-self" principles, for indeed his work was self-supporting, self-governing and self-propagating. Ironically, it was his spiritual (not political) opposition to the government's *Three-Self Protestant Patriotic Movement* that resulted in his imprisonment.

In 1937 his famous church The Christian Tabernacle was built in Peking. There the form of worship was as unsophisticated as the architecture was spartan. There wasn't even a choir lest it foster pride or be Christian entertainment to distract worshipers. Wang's position from his youth, on which he based his preaching, was "I accept all that is written in Scripture, and what I cannot find written there I shall leave aside." Wang himself never accepted ordination as a clergyman, always insisting on being called "Mr." and functioning only as one of the church's preaching brothers.

Just before the Communist "liberation" in 1949, Wang refused to sign a manifesto which demanded first loyalty to the Communist party and the declaration that the Christian church in China had been a tool of imperialism. He considered the Christian leaders who were being used by the government to promote this manifesto to be liberals and compromisers and publically denounced them. (Some of the messages in this volume were written at this time and with such persons in mind.) When *The Three-Self Patriotic Movement* followed on the heels of the manifesto, Wang also denounced this as a compromising body, knowing well that the ax would come down upon him sooner or later.

The ax did fall. Angered and fearing his influence, *The Three-Self Movement* initiated accusation meetings against Wang. Even after the trial and public humiliation he continued his fervent preaching and criticism of any compromise. Unable any longer to get his Christian magazine prepared by any printer, Wang set up his own printing press and painstakingly set his own type. (During this period Wang wrote the remainder of the bold articles selected for this book, exhorting himself as well as his flock to stand fast for the Lord even unto death.) On August 7, 1955, after midnight, Pastor and Mrs. Wang, with a number of Chrisians from The Tabernacle, were arrested, bound and taken to jail. Wang was given a fifteen-year sentence on the grounds that he was an anti-revolutionary. Within a few weeks his church was closed down.

God allowed His faithful servant to be tested on the very truths he had so courageously proclaimed. Under intense psychological harassment, brainwashing, verbal abuse, debate, prolonged physical exhaustion—all designed to break mental competency—Pastor Wang broke down. Under duress he signed a document admitting guilt for anti-revolutionary activities and was released to read his confession in public before an elated gathering of *The Three-Self Movement*.

Crushed by the traumatic ordeal and how his confession had affected and scattered his flock, Wang was reported to have wandered about saying, "I am Peter," and sometimes "I am Judas." Eventually, after regaining his health and mental balance, he returned to the authorities and retracted his confession, maintaining that it had been forced from him. Wang was immediately jailed again and his sentence extended to life imprisonment.

Then followed a twenty-one year parenthesis of silence in which little was known of Pastor Wang except that he was thought to be still alive and reported determined to be faithful to the Lord, even until death this time. His wife, Deborah, was held in a prison elsewhere and they did not see one another or their son during those terrible years.

Mrs. Wang was released in 1977 for health reasons and Pastor Wang was released in 1980, both with their Christian faith stronger than ever, rejoicing in the Lord, purified by the fires of suffering though broken in health and aged. Both were nearly blind and Pastor Wang was eighty percent deaf.

The name given Wang at birth meant "iron." Strong as iron is, it can break. And Pastor Wang did break under intense pressure early in his imprisonment, though he hurried to repent. Surely God forgave him as He had forgiven Peter the apostle who denied Jesus three times. But God went to work on this man of iron to turn him into steel...through more than two decades of isolation which gave am-ple opportunity for him to practice what he had preached. Through his suffering God stamped His own image more deeply on Wang's character. Now Pastor Wang often quotes for visitors one of the verses which upheld him year after year in prison, "Therefore we do not lose heart, but though our outer man is decaying, yet our inner man is being renewed day by day. For momentary, light affliction is producing for us an eternal weight of glory far beyond all comparison" (2 Corinthians 4:16,17).

His Writings—A Trumpet Call for Battle

As Pastor Wang Ming-dao became mature in Christian experience and the study of God's Word, he became well known for his incisive messages. They demanded repentance from sin and a practical, clean, transparent, daily walk with God.

But Wang always first opened himself up to allow God's Spirit to cut away sin from his own heart and life. From his conversion as a youth he had fiercely hated sin and longed for holiness. "When I committed sin I was greatly distressed and chided myself," he confesses. "When I see other people sin, I am very pained. All kinds of sin are apparent even in the church, and it fills me with righteous anger." In his own words, "God sent me on the one hand to be a trumpet call to the world and on the other hand to be a trumpet call to the church... to expose darkness, corruption, depravity and unrighteousness and to summon men without delay to repent." By his own admission he did so with fear and trembling, knowing that he would draw opposition to himself for speaking and writing so openly against sin.

His writings are described as "straightforwardly correcting evil without sparing people's feelings." But like the prophet Jeremiah (20:8,9), he could not refrain from speaking out. He believed it better to offend people than fail to lead them to the Lord. The more he spoke or wrote, the greater was his courage and power to rebuke sins and hold up a high standard of morality. No respecter of persons, he directed his preaching equally against rich and poor, prestigious and lowly, nominal Christians, Chinese church leaders and Western missionaries.

Inevitably, many did oppose and reject Pastor Wang, calling him proud and ultra-critical. But like the prophets of the Old Testament and Jesus Himself, he never compromised the pure message of God's Word. Yet it was his attitude of speaking the truth in love that tempered the pain of the remedial surgeon's knife, the sharper-than-a-two-edged-sword Word of God that he wielded. Referring to the content of his own messages, Pastor Wang called them plain and faithful expositions battling for God's truth as a soldier of the cross. Of his unembellished speaking and writing style, Pastor Wang admitted that he was not eloquent but that he had to depend entirely upon God's gift for communicating in power.

With the growth of Pastor Wang's popularity as a fearless exponent of God's Word, the demand for his messages in a more permanent form gave rise to his mimeographing some of them in the early days. Later he established a magazine called *The Spiritual Food Quarterly*, and since 1926 it has been avidly read by Chinese Christians not only in China but all over the world. The magazine articles were then compiled into more than twenty books in Chinese. Some were published by Pastor Wang, others by various publishers outside of China who collected them while Pastor Wang was in prison. These writings have blessed and challenged Chinese readers but English readers have remained deprived of their richness. To fill this lack we are presenting this initial volume with great assurance that Pastor Wang's messages in translation will equally edify English readers.

The chapters in this book are articles specifically selected by the translator and editor from those preached and written by Pastor Wang in the period just prior to his imprisonment, before the mid 1950's. They are compiled from various of the Chinese books of his collected messages. The topics are especially relevant to encourage Christian believers worldwide to stand courageously for the Faith. Although delivered with the church in China in mind originally, they are greatly significant to the church of today in the West, in so-called restricted lands where the gospel is prohibited from being freely preached, and wherever the forces of darkness are clashing ever more fiercely with God's Light in the unseen spiritual conflict.

To pinpoint the historical setting in which they were written, it was after the establishment of the Communist regime in China in 1949, during the mounting pressures against imperialism, foreignism, and religious institutions in China in general. The period was pre-Cultural Revolution, which was launched around 1966. Pastor Wang was in prison for its duration and released after the death of Party Chairman Mao Tse-tung and after the normalization of diplomatic relations between the United States and the People's Republic of China in 1979. Humanly speaking, it seems such a waste that we have no writings from Pastor Wang during his long years of imprisonment. Though allowed paper and pen, he was not permitted to keep anything he wrote, so those writings are lost to the world. Since his release, his failing eyesight and fragile health have prevented any further writing. Nevertheless, after Pastor Wang was released from prison at nearly eighty years of age and asked what message he would like to send to the outside world, he proclaimed the same uncompromising stand as before his twenty-three year incarceration. The trumpet sounded again with clear conviction: "Stand firm in your faith; live the Christian life which you confess. Then God will use you wherever you are."

During personal visits with Pastor Wang and his wife in China, the translator and editor have assured themselves that Pastor Wang's faith is undaunted and untarnished and his convictions and messages would be the same as reflected in these chapters were he allowed to preach and write today—rebuking and exposing the current sins of the church and the world, especially of nominal Christians and unfaithful leadership in the church wherever the Body of Christ is found. Bear in mind that these messages are not theological treatises but down-to-earth preaching.

After a nearly verbatim translation as a base, editing consisted primarily of clarifying syntax, refraining from undue paraphrasing and endeavoring to keep the typical terse flavor and thought patterns of Pastor Wang. His style reflects the delight in long lists of virtues and sins, questions to the reader, and a reasoning, logical approach to his theme. The only liberty taken was to summarize the lengthy Scripture passages which he usually quoted within his articles and to footnote the Scripture texts at the end of the chapters so as not to distract the reader's progression of thought. Therefore what the reader reads is what Pastor Wang wrote, and it is offered as his own burden and concern. Each chapter is a separate message, though the themes are interwoven and build one upon the other. In these topics he seems to prophetically chronicle situations that subsequently unfolded around him. Readers are invited to read between the lines, knowing what happened in his life after their writing. Even the man of God who determined "never to declare that white was black," (see Chapter 1) did so under intense persecution.

Pastor Wang claims that whenever he preached or wrote articles he was himself reproved, comforted and encouraged from the Lord. The translator and editor enthusiastically echo this confession for themselves as they have worked on his writings. With the publisher, we earnestly hope and pray that readers will be similarly challenged to holy, practical and uncompromising Christian living—and earnest prayer for the persecuted church worldwide.

Translator: Theodore Choy
Editor: Leona Frances Choy

一

在小事上忠心

1

Nitty-gritty Faithfulness

"*He who is faithful in a very little thing is faithful also in much*" —Luke 16:10a.

"He who is faithful in a very little thing is faithful also in much; and he who is unrighteous in a very little thing is unrighteous also in much."[1] This declaration by our Lord Jesus contains a very precious and important truth. He tells us why, among those who are saved, the disciples of Christ, there are some who live a noble and holy life; and on the other hand, why some live a very dirty and contemptible life so that people can hardly believe they are Christians. The statement informs us that some march forward on the spiritual battlefield, fight victoriously with the enemy, hold their banner high and get ever stronger and braver; but others, when confronted by Satan in battle, retreat and fail all the time. Many think that this difference among Christians is due to some very large matters. When we come down to the nitty-gritty, however, it is not because of big things but because of small things. A believer must forsake the *smallest* sins and then he may live a holy and noble life. A believer must stand fast and not give in to Satan in the *small* things; then he can go on to win the greatest victory. If he neglects the smallest sin, sooner or later he will fall into a large one. If a believer gives in to Satan in a small matter, sooner or later he will face a catastrophic failure. At the time he was committing a so-called minor sin he might never have dreamed that he would ever be capable of committing a major sin. But in reality, he was preparing well for committing the gross sin. When he gave an inch to Satan, he certainly did not expect to surrender all the way to Satan, but he unknowingly had already paved the way to full surrender.

In the Bible, God never teaches us to surrender to Satan; rather, He instructs us not to give Satan any opportunity.[2] Satan does not fret that down the line we might not surrender to him; he is worried only that we won't give him the first opportunity. For if given that one inch or that one step, he is sure that sooner or later we will surrender. Certainly no Christian willingly surrenders to Satan, but so many do give Satan an opportunity. Though they had not the slightest intention of surrender in the beginning, yet many have finally submitted to his power. God knew of this danger, so He taught us through Paul not to grant Satan that first opportunity. He instructed us even further: "Resist the devil and he will flee from you."[3] The way to deal with Satan is to stand against him, resist and refuse him. If we don't obey God's word, but try to employ some other method of our own to deal with Satan, we will certainly be defeated by him.

The devil always wants us to emphasize the larger things and neglect the smaller. He persistently clouds our minds into thinking that we shouldn't commit serious sins but a few insignificant ones don't make any difference. If we listen to his suggestions and reasoning, he will lead us step by step toward those larger ones. And since we have already followed him in the little sins, it becomes easier and easier to commit greater sins. Consequently, not only are our sins getting bigger and bigger, but also more and more numerous. Gradually our sensitivity toward sin becomes less and less. Finally we fall headlong into the large sins and really get into trouble. Satan's

Nitty-gritty Faithfulness

trick to hurt us has been successful... and we will be facing destruction.

We all know that a levee along a river can break when summer rains have been intense and much water has poured down from the mountains. As the water in the river rises higher and higher, it threatens to flood the banks. Then the farmland, the homes, people and cattle will be inundated and destroyed. Those who live on the banks of rivers want to prevent flooding, so they build levees to prevent the water from getting out of bounds. Those levees should be free from any leaks. If just a trickle of water begins to spout from a small opening, the strength of the water will soon enlarge the opening. In a short time the levee will break and the flood will cause a great disaster.

In our human life, sin is frightening and powerful—like a great flood in the summer. We must prevent the flood by securing the levee and not allowing even a trickle of sin to come into our lives. When we commit a small sin, it is just like neglecting a small hole in the levee. If we don't plug it immediately, before long it will result in a great disaster. Those who are responsible for watching for danger along the levee do not ignore even a very small leak. But, sorry to say, so many Christians do not pay attention to the small sins in their lives. Because they neglect those, considering them only insignificant leaks in the levee, their whole lives are destroyed.

Spiritual victory is obtained by being watchful in small matters. If a small temptation comes and you can overcome it, your faith, courage and strength will be increased. Then when you face a stronger temptation, you are fortified and can be victorious more easily. By contrast, when you encounter a small temptation and fail, your faith, courage and strength will be reduced and you will become weaker. Then when you face a larger temptation, you are already guaranteed to fail.

Some people have a wrong perspective. They say that it is not worthwhile to sacrifice for a small matter. When an important issue comes along, of course they will be willing to make a sacrifice—*that* will be worthwhile. But such a view is clearly the suggestion of Satan trying to deceive us. Suppose that when a battalion of soldiers met an attack by only a couple dozen foot soldiers the commander were to say, "Oh never mind, they are so few that it is not really worthwhile to waste our efforts and manpower on a confrontation with them. We can just temporarily give up this little bit of frontier and withdraw to a safer place. We will wait until there are hundreds or thousands of the enemy, and then we will rise up and fight with them. That will be worthwhile!" If anyone heard a commander-in-chief say something like that, he would certainly be shocked. We would wonder whether the man was a coward, just ignorant, or perhaps might have accepted a bribe from the enemy and was preparing to surrender the whole territory eventually. If he was fearful or ignorant he should immediately be removed from his important position. If he was indeed preparing to abandon the territory, then he should be charged with collaboration with the enemy. Everyone knows that when any of the enemy attack, they must be dealt with immediately, no matter how many or few. When a larger contingent attacks, if the few were not dealt with, the whole army will capitulate to the enemy.

Suppose a piece of white paper is laid before us and most people declare, "It is black," but I insist that it is white. That will surely disturb those others and invite their ill feelings. Some friends might advise, "Don't make an issue of it. What does it matter if everyone is saying that the paper is black; go ahead and agree with them and keep peace. If you do so, there is nothing important at stake; so why should you stir up opposition against yourself? Why not peacefully coexist with others and gain greater opportunities to serve them and witness for the Lord? Wouldn't that be wonderful? But if you persist in saying that the piece of paper is white, you will not only irritate others, you will disrupt all harmony with them and lose the chance to help them. And because you make yourself out to be so different from others, they will not respect the God whom you serve and there will be a great loss all around." This kind of argument or logic may sound quite reasonable and attractive, but if you analyze it carefully you will know it is based on a principle which *looks* right but is *completely wrong*. The problem is that this approach easily confuses people so that, without being aware of it, they fall into big trouble. If you say a white paper is black, surely, according to man's way of thinking, that is not an important issue. But according to

Nitty-gritty Faithfulness

Biblical teaching, it is very serious. If we follow human logic we are contradicting what Jesus taught us. He said that our words should be "Yes" or "No," and if we go beyond plain words such as these, it is evil.[4]

May I ask, If this piece of paper is really white—even though others are willing to say it is black—is it not clearly against the standards and commands of the Lord for me to agree with the wrong statement? If a man says he is a disciple of Jesus but does not obey His command, do you think that is important? Our Lord added a statement about unclear or compromising words that is very important: "...and anything beyond these is of evil." Don't you see? To speak the words "black" or "white" does not seem to be such an important matter, but if we say that a white paper is black when it is not, it is *very* serious. When we say that, we lie and are violating the command of the Lord. That is from the evil one. Then as Christians we will be guilty of a major sin. If we persist in saying that this is not important, I don't know what *is* important in this world!

Maybe someone will say, "If I should say that a white sheet of paper is black, at most I myself only speak a lie. This will not hurt anyone nor disgrace the name of God. On the contrary," they reason, "if I agree with their false statement, it might remove people's dislike of me. Then I can live in closer harmony with others and be able to help them because I bear no ill will against anyone nor they against me. God will be glorified. Wouldn't that be wonderful? I cannot understand why you insist on saying that if I do agree with them it would be such a very serious sin."

Let me tell you this. The committing of any sin is consequential, for by every sin we hurt someone and also disgrace our Lord. The only question is whether the fallout will come sooner or happen later. Let me ask you, Since it is clear that this is a white sheet of paper, why do you want to say that it is black? If no one had mentioned that it was black, you would not have said that it was black without a reason, would you? It is because many people are saying that it is black...and so you join them and say that it is black. Obviously you are afraid of offending other people and therefore are willing to utter an untruth like saying that a white paper is black. Because it seems such a small matter in your sight, you are unwilling to take a stand lest you offend another person over it.

If a big temptation comes along, do you think you will suddenly have the courage to overcome *it*? Today, because you are afraid to offend another person over such a seemingly small matter, and agree to a lie, someday many people may say that a certain innocent person is evil—and will you have the courage to say that he is innocent when you know that he truly is? Today, if you have the courage to say that a white paper is white, tomorrow you will have the courage to say that an innocent person is innocent. Surely you would not say that an innocent person is guilty just because you are afraid of offending the people who say that he is evil, would you? If you treat a person dishonestly because of your fear of offending people, you will undoubtedly end up denying the Lord. In that hour you will be surprised at yourself that you could ever have fallen into such a serious failure as that. If I can hurt an innocent person, then I should not be shocked that I am capable of even denying and betraying my gracious Lord. It would not surprise me a bit that sooner or later I could utterly fail, and the damage would be irreparable, if I began by calling a white piece of paper black.

What stand then shall I take? It is simple. When I see that a paper is white, I will definitely never say that it is black. Actually, I do not need to say anything about it and can keep my mouth shut *if the issue is not brought up*. But if it has become an issue and you want me to follow the majority and say that it is black, I will absolutely never, never do it! I am not afraid of offending someone because of this, nor do I fear to suffer loss or risk any danger. I must fight for the truth—black is black and white is white! Even if I lost my life for it, I would count it as a most glorious, valuable act. If I am unwilling to say that a white paper is black, and I lose my life over that, I believe that my death would be just as great and glorious and worthwhile as the death of Stephen or James or Peter or Paul. And I would have an equal reward from the Lord. Also, I truly understand that I must overcome in this small thing before I can overcome in great things. Today, if I determine not to say that the white paper is black, in the future I will not hurt innocent people nor will I betray my Lord. Today, I will insist that this white paper *is* white. Then in the future I can stand fast for my faith.

Nitty-gritty Faithfulness

Spiritual battles are like earthly battles. Every time you overcome, your courage increases. The next time it will be easier to succeed. On the other hand, once you fail, your courage diminishes and a future battle will become more difficult for you. You will soon retreat step by step until your whole army is wiped out or captured. We are soldiers under the banner of Jesus Christ in a spiritual battle and we can only advance and never retreat! We can only stand fast on our ground! We cannot surrender one small inch! And if the Lord commands us to do something, no matter how small, we must do it. Whatever the Lord is not pleased with, no matter how small, we must by all means avoid it. We must treat the small thing and the large thing with the same importance. We must see the same frightening danger in the small sin that we recognize in the great sin. We should never, never be deceived by Satan to view the small thing as less important or of no significance. The Lord has spoken this very important truth most clearly: "He who is faithful in a very little thing is faithful also in much; and he who is unrighteous in a very little thing is unrighteous also in much."

- - - - - - -

Background verses used in the above text:

[1] Luke 16:10
[2] Ephesians 4:27
[3] James 4:7
[4] Matthew 5:37

二　　順服神，順服人？

2

Obey God or Men?

> *Let every person be in subjection to the governing authorities*
> —Romans 13:1a.

Are Christians obliged to be subject to the laws of this world and to men who are in authority? If we affirm this, why were Peter and John not subject to the high priest and the Jewish officials in the days of the early church? They were commanded ". . . not to speak or teach at all in the name of Jesus."[1] But the apostles did not obey these established authorities. The first time they were forbidden to preach the gospel, they retorted, "Whether it is right in the sight of God to give heed to you rather than to God, you be the judge; for we cannot stop speaking what we have seen and heard."[2] The second time they were forbidden, they declared, "We must obey God rather than men."[3] After they were beaten and released, did they still preach Jesus? Yes, even more diligently! "And every day, in the temple and from house to house, they kept right on teaching and preaching Jesus as the Christ."[4]

If we take the position that Christians should not obey the laws of this world and those who are in places of authority, then why did the apostle Paul teach the church: "Let every person be in subjection to the governing authorities"?[5] And why did he also say: "Remind them to be subject to rulers, to authorities, to be obedient, to be ready for every good deed..."?[6] And again, why did Peter write: "Submit yourselves for the Lord's sake to every human institution, whether to a king as the one in authority, or to governors as sent by him,... for such is the will of God..."?[7]

If it is right and proper to be subject to law and to those in authority, the apostles then shouldn't have resisted the command of the high priest, the Jewish officials and the elders. Neither should they have said, "We must obey God rather than men." All the more so after they were actually publicly forbidden to preach Jesus. If it is not right to obey the authorities of this world, then the apostles should not have written these portions which teach the saints to do so, nor should they have provided examples by their own actions.

I would resolve the question thus: First, we should obey God. Second, within the scope of not being contrary to God's commandments, we should also obey all the regulations and dictates of men. But if the regulations and decrees of men come into conflict with God's commands, then we have no alternative but to disobey men and obey only God. So Christians should obey man, not because they are afraid of punishment, but because they fear God and God has commanded us to obey those in authority. Therefore, if the regulations and laws conflict with God's commands, it is obvious that we cannot obey them.

The fact that the apostles did not obey the high priest, the Jewish officials and elders, is a case in point. To preach the gospel of Jesus was clearly the commission and command of God. The high priest and his cohorts forbade them to do so. There was no question but that they should not obey this order and so they did not. Under such circumstances they stood on God's ground and said, "We must obey God rather than men."

Some Christians have misunderstood the apostles' statement. They have interpreted it to mean that if we are to obey God, then we should not obey anyone else. So they have applied it to disobeying parents in their home and teachers in school, not observing regulations or directives. At work, they take unauthorized time off for their own pleasure. If someone attempts to call them down, they maintain they are Christians and are only obliged to obey God and not men. The conduct of such people not only invites many problems and does damage to themselves, but also reflects disgrace on God. Such a wrong attitude needs correction. Those people need to pay attention to the teaching of the Scriptures, "Submit yourselves for the Lord's sake to every human institution."

Wherever he is, the Christian should be exemplary in obedience to all laws and regulations. He should not wait until someone rebukes or corrects him before he consents to obey laws and regulations. If this becomes necessary, it should be to his disgrace. He should personally pay much attention to respecting all authority conscientiously, obeying each and every law. If he did not know about one or somehow neglected one inadvertently, and so transgressed a certain rule or regulation, after it has been pointed out to him he should confess his mistake immediately and joyfully. He should accept the correction of others and quickly amend his ways. By all means he should never cover up his errors or be unwilling to admit a mistake. Worse, he should not get angry or speak unreasonable words, becoming rude or disrespectful.

How can we make such teaching practical in our daily lives and work? Suppose a Christian is a student at school. Whether he is in the lecture hall, classroom, dormitory, dining hall, on the field or in the library, he should strictly observe all rules. He should never be late for class, never speak loudly so as to disturb others who are silently studying, never turn on the light without good reason after it is time for lights out. He should not disturb others who are sleeping. At mealtime he should never push ahead in line. He should not deface buildings or damage equipment. He should always respect teachers and study his lessons diligently.

A Christian teacher should prepare his lessons well and be diligent in instruction, both at school and in his own home. He should regard his students as his own children, teaching them patiently and in an orderly manner.

A Christian working in an office should be prompt and should never waste time on the job nor engage in his private affairs on company time. Jobs which are committed to him should be taken care of personally, not turned over to others. What can be done today should not be put off until tomorrow. Unless there is an emergency, he should not take extra days off. He should not make excuses for neglecting work given him by his supervisors.

A Christian who works in a factory should be scrupulous about his time, be careful with the goods he handles, obey his superiors, be diligent in his work, not only while people are watching but even when no one is around.

A Christian doctor should treat his patients as his own loved ones at home. He should carefully and thoroughly diagnose the patient, never be careless or brush off the patient's complaints lightly. A Christian nurse should wholeheartedly care for the sick. She should never waste time while on duty or neglect the needs of the patients. If she is on the night shift, she should manage to get enough sleep in the daytime so that she can be fully alert when giving medication to the patients, so that she will make no mistake and endanger a patient. When she speaks to those who are ill, she should be courteous and gentle.

A Christian businessman should never pass off inferior products as the best products or present a stale product as fresh. He should never put on a false price or cheat country folks, strangers or foreigners. He should never use deceitful yardsticks or measures. He should never try to get out of proper taxation.

A Christian who takes a journey or goes sightseeing should pay attention to posted notices of rules. He should enter from stated entrances and come out from proper exits. He should never touch anything that is indicated untouchable nor enter places that are marked out-of-bounds. He should never walk on the grass or pick forbidden flowers or fruits from the trees or deface public property. When a Christian drives a car he should observe all the rules of traffic and obey the traffic police.

Having said the above, I must nevertheless state that under certain circumstances we should not submit to man. Such occasions would be when man's system or commands conflict with God's commands or principles. Then we can only obey God and not man. Certainly children should obey their parents, but if the parents require their children to lie, then children should not obey their parents. Students should obey their teachers, but if teachers lead the students in ancestor worship, the students should not obey the teachers. Christians should obey their job supervisors, but if they are forbidden to pray, read the Bible, join Christian meetings and witness for the Lord Jesus on their own time, then they should not obey the authorities. When man's system and commands do not conflict with the will of God, Christians should be obedient. But if man's system and commands conflict with God's commands and the truths of the Bible, then we should absolutely never obey. At such a time we should take our stand on what the apostles said, "We must obey God rather than men."

Christians should obey all the rules and regulations of man and those in authority. But Christians should also obey God's will, which is to fellowship with believers, serve God with others in the church, keep the church holy, witness for the Lord and spread the gospel of salvation. All these should absolutely not be interfered with by anyone. For the cause of *freedom to do these things,* we should count no sacrifice too costly. We should follow the courageous and firm stand of the apostles in these matters.

After the Lord Jesus ascended into heaven, the Jewish political and religious leaders used their thundering madness and power to try to eliminate the gospel and the church of Christ. But because of the courageous and firm stand of the apostles, the gospel was nevertheless spread abroad and the church was established. The believers who followed also took courage and stood their ground, spreading the gospel all over the world. We, in turn, heard the gospel in China and many of us have accepted salvation, also becoming God's children and inheriting everlasting life.

Some have asked me what path the church should take today. I answer: Unquestionably, the path of the apostles. That is, follow the footsteps of the apostles by imitating their courageous and firm stand, not being afraid of any threatenings, not holding life dear, being faithful unto death, not pleasing men. Even while meeting resistance, we should still preach the gospel and teach God's words to people. The one who can do this will be blessed by God and used by God. He may indeed meet what the apostles met in persecution, but he will also accomplish what the apostles accomplished. Without doubt, God's glory and great power will be manifested through him just as it was manifested in that day through the apostles.

It is lamentable that many Christian leaders use the principle of obedience to man's rules and submission to man's authority to cover up their cowardice and failure. They thus deceive many believers who don't fully understand the truths of the Bible. This results in the faith of the church and the ministry being subordinated to the rule of men and man's authority. The truth then becomes obscured, the Bible misinterpreted, the foundations of the church undermined and the flock scattered. The church and the gospel of Christ are thereby degraded and put on a lower plane than compliance to men's rules and submitting to human authority.

These foundational and precious things are so lightly surrendered by some so-called servants of God! How can such Christian leaders then escape the wrath of God?

- - - - - - -

Background verses used in the above text:

[1] Acts 4:18
[2] Acts 4:19,20
[3] Acts 5:29-32
[4] Acts 5:42
[5] Romans 13:1
[6] Titus 3:1
[7] 1 Peter 2:13-15

三　　預備受苦

3

Preparation for Suffering

> *To you it has been granted for Christ's sake, not only to believe in Him, but also to suffer for His sake* —Philippians 1:29.

"Therefore, since Christ has suffered in the flesh, arm yourselves also with the same purpose, because he who has suffered in the flesh has ceased from sin, so as to live the rest of the time in the flesh no longer for the lusts of men, but for the will of God."[1]

I would like to point out that the word "arm," as a verb, is not limited to meaning the using of a weapon to attack an enemy; it can also mean the putting on of armor to protect yourself from being injured by the enemy. The apostle Peter, who has brought this to our attention, had suffered a most serious defeat by Satan. When his Master was brought to judgment in the court of the high priest, Peter denied Him three times. He not only denied that Jesus was his Master, he even swore, "I don't know that man."[2] Why did he fail to such an extreme? The reason was his fear of being arrested by the Jews and possibly suffering as his Master was about to suffer. He was not prepared to suffer at that time. In other words, he had not "armed himself" with the spirit of suffering; therefore he was defeated by his enemy.

Not long afterward he saw his Master accomplish the great task of redemption for the human race. Through His suffering Christ overcame the devil and the power of death, rising again from the dead. Peter saw his Lord *triumph through suffering*. Then he clearly understood that his own failure was because he was afraid to suffer. His experience made him fully comprehend that the only way to overcome the enemy's threat and attacks was to "arm himself with the spirit of suffering." Therefore, after the Lord Jesus' ascension, Peter was ready to suffer daily.

A few weeks after this, the religious leaders of the Jews arrested Peter and his companions in the temple and forbade them to preach in Jesus' name. But after they were warned and released, they continued to preach with boldness.[3] When they were once again arrested and brought to trial, Peter and the others did not back down but retorted, "We must obey God rather than men."[4] Why was Peter so brave and strong at this time compared with the time when he denied the Lord in the court of the high priest? It was almost as if he were a different person. One reason was that he had received the power of the Holy Spirit at Pentecost, along with the other apostles and followers of Jesus. The other reason was that he now was "armed with the spirit of suffering." Previously he had been afraid of suffering, so he had lied and denied his Lord in order to escape the suffering—and had fallen into lamentable failure. But now he was ready to suffer; he did not try to avoid danger. So the enemy could no longer overcome him. He had continual victories. He had deeply apprehended this truth through his own experience; therefore he could encourage the church, saying, "Therefore, since Christ has suffered in the flesh, arm yourselves also with the same purpose."

Peter continues by declaring that the one who has suffered in the flesh has ceased from sin. These words clearly show us that God permits us to suffer for our own good. The experience of many

Preparation for Suffering 31

believers confirms these words. There are many sins we need to get rid of through suffering. Only as we suffer can we clearly see the faults and failures in our lives and be led to deeply humble ourselves and repent. Then our dross can be purified and our rough spots be made smooth. Look at those Christians with the highest morality and lives of holiness. How many have not been through much suffering?

Our flesh keeps us from obeying God's will. Satan and the world he controls also obstruct us from doing God's will. Satan and the world he controls use all sorts of things to threaten us. Our flesh responds to the voice of Satan within us, leading us to think about the possibility of danger, loss, disgrace and hardship if we do God's will. If we do not arm ourselves with the spirit of suffering, we will not dare to obey God's will. But if we have prepared beforehand and armed ourselves with the spirit of suffering, then, when Satan, the world and our flesh come unitedly against us, we will answer them, "Suffering? Good! I have already prepared for it. I welcome it as if I welcomed my dear friend." When we have such a spirit, and declare it, the invasion of the enemy will utterly fail. We will also "live the rest of the time in the flesh no longer for the lusts of men, but for the will of God."

Some Christians do not have victory during suffering, so they fall; but more often, Christians are afraid even of the threats Satan uses. He says to them, "If you confess the name of the Lord before people who oppose God, saying that you are a follower of Jesus, you will meet with many attacks and ridicule. If you persist in what you believe, there will be absolutely no retreat and you will endanger your entire future. If you want to be an absolutely sincere person, determined not to lie, you will meet unimaginable trouble. If you never take any money dishonestly, you will suffer hunger and cold. If you don't try to win the unbelievers' sympathy and understanding, you will have no standing in this world. If you live wholly according to the teachings of the Bible, trying to please God and not men, you will become the enemy of all the people. If you want to imitate Christ in everything, you will surely meet death just as He died."

Yes, *Satan* puts such thoughts into our minds. He whispers many frightening words into believers' ears, and if they allow them to enter into their hearts they are frightened and trembling. Under such circumstances they do not dare either to stand fast or to fully obey God's will and attack. Of course, these trembling ones do not intend to fail *utterly;* they are not ready to *surrender* to Satan. They are only considering retreating to a certain point, thinking there will still be time to negotiate some kind of compromise. They do not realize that when they retreat from Satan, Satan will again and again advance to attack. It is inevitable that they will gradually be defeated and finally become the captives of Satan.

Such failure is a natural consequence. When an army is in battle, it can only *attack* the enemy. Even if it should be unable to advance, at least it must defend its own territory. It should never consider retreat or prepare to do so. If an army retreats, its territory is diminished and the enemy force increases. After the first retreat, the second will follow easily. Today a foot, the next day a mile; then it will be three miles, five, ten, twenty—a full retreat. The end is unimaginable.

Of course we should always be ready to suffer, but whether suffering will befall us or not depends on the will of God. If He sees that our suffering will be for our own good, He will let it come. Otherwise, even if we are ready to suffer, it will not come upon us. The apostle James was killed by Herod, who then proceeded to arrest Peter, intending to execute him also. But God sent an angel to lead Peter out of prison, delivering him from the hand of Herod.[5] Could not God have saved James as well as Peter? Is God a respecter of persons? God saw that James' ministry was finished and brought James into Glory through the hand of Herod. God still had much work to commit to Peter, so he was delivered from prison by the angel. It was not that James was less fortunate than Peter. Peter's deliverance from prison was no proof that God dealt more favorably with Peter than with James. God had two different plans for them, so their lot was also different. It is useless to ask God how He plans to deal with each of us. If God wants us to suffer death like James, we should praise Him. If He wants us to be treated like Peter, we should also praise Him. We should not try to choose either one of the two lots. Neither have we the right to ask God to let us know what our future will be. We should only be ever ready to suffer. Let us "arm ourselves with the spirit of suffering" so that we may "live the rest of our time

Preparation for Suffering

in the flesh no longer for the lusts of men, but for the will of God." Many Christians, when in danger, suffering trial or hearing unfavorable news, are anxious to know how the future will turn out, whether good or bad. This is a very unhealthy attitude. Personally, I will not ask God to let me know what my future will be. I only know that, according to God's will, I'll run the race set before me today and do the work I must do today. I will not ask God to let me know whether my future is bright or full of shadows—nor do I want to know. If I knew that my future was to be smooth and prosperous, I'm afraid I would tend to be careless and fall into temptation. If I knew that my future held hardship and persecution, I'm afraid I would be fearful and anxious, and the devil would have an opportunity to harm me. I don't wish to know what I will encounter. I can only "arm myself with the spirit of suffering" so that I may meet *whatever* befalls me.

There's a negative mind-set that we should all avoid: We like to hear news that is frightening or alarming, and after hearing it we like to pass the word on to others. We should rather be eager to hear only words that strengthen our faith and encourage us to go forward. Through the words of our mouths we can strengthen others and tell them to trust in God. We should not listen to the negative report of the ten spies who came back from scouting in the Promised Land. If we do, we will hold back and cry aloud; we will murmur and moan that we want to return to Egypt, and thus we will invite the curse of God. We should rather hear the word of faith from Joshua and Caleb. We shouldn't be bearers of bad tidings, repeating words that shake people's faith so that they become fearful and weak. Like Joshua and Caleb we should encourage people to look to the power and promises of God, advising them not to look at outward circumstances. Don't set your mind on negative people and things. We should say to timid persons, "The *Lord* is with us; be not afraid of *them.*" If we do that, it is honoring God. Then God will honor us and bless us like Joshua and Caleb. If we spread bad news, repeating words that weaken people's faith so that they become afraid, we do harm to those who hear us and we bring the wrath of God upon ourselves. We will be just like the ten who were struck dead with a plague for bringing a bad report concerning the land.[6]

Some may say, "Since we are prepared to bear suffering, what is wrong in listening to threatening news so we can get ready ahead of time?" You must understand that being prepared to suffer is the fruit of our trust and godly obedience, but words from those bringing bad news are Satan's darts to the intent that we should become fearful and lose our faith and disobey God. If we just by chance hear people bringing bad news, God will surely protect us so that we need not be weakened. But if we constantly are tuned in to hear negative words or if we go out of our way to listen for such news, that is enough to prove that we still have a fearful heart toward suffering. If we have that kind of spirit, how can we talk about having "armed ourselves with the spirit of suffering"?

Satan attacks Christians without ceasing. The spiritual battle becomes more and more fierce. Let us obey the teaching of God given through the apostle: "Arm yourselves with the spirit of suffering" to stand against Satan and his hosts until the day we obtain the great victory and sing the triumphal song!

- - - - - - -

Background verses used in the above text:
[1] 1 Peter 4:1,2
[2] Mark 14:66-72
[3] Acts 4:1-31
[4] Acts 5:29-32
[5] Acts 12:1-10
[6] Numbers 13:1—14:38

四

那聽不見的聲音

4

The Missing Voice

"Everywhere I send you, you shall go, and all that I command you, you shall speak. Do not be afraid of them, for I am with you to deliver you," declares the Lord —Jeremiah 1:7c,8.

Only one episode about Micaiah is recorded in the Bible, in 1 Kings 22 and 2 Chronicles 18. Although we don't know anything about his birth or his death, through this isolated incident we know he was a great and unique prophet. Because he was so faithful, courageous and fearless that he would not bow under the authority of King Ahab, nor seek to please men, he spoke what the Lord wanted him to speak. When the lying spirit entered into the mouths of the four hundred other prophets, he alone was perceptive and alert to see things which the others did not see and speak things the other prophets dared not speak.

From this record we can see that Micaiah must have been a well-known prophet, more famous than the four hundred other prophets. For when Ahab summoned the four hundred, Jehoshaphat asked, "Is there not yet a prophet of the Lord here, that we may inquire of him?" Since there were already four hundred prophets of the Lord standing before them both, how could Jehoshaphat determine that there was still one missing? He must have already known about a certain one who usually spoke differently from the rest of the prophets. He paid no attention to the four hundred but his eyes scanned the crowd for Micaiah. When he heard the four hundred all declaring the same message, immediately he guessed that Micaiah was missing. Otherwise there would have been one word of counsel that was different from the rest. Consequently he asked Ahab whether there was still another prophet to be heard from.

Jehoshaphat's suspicions were right. Ahab answered, "There is yet one man by whom we may inquire of the Lord, but I hate him, because he does not prophesy good concerning me, but evil." Since that prophet had already incurred Ahab's hatred, when all the other prophets were summoned Micaiah was deliberately left off the invitation list.

Ahab, as king of the nation, had full authority to either kill or let live. It would seem that Micaiah was very foolish to antagonize the king by continually speaking negatively when he could have gotten along much better by speaking to please him. According to an ancient saying, "A wise man protects his body." If that is true, Micaiah seems to have been a number-one fool. Was he really? Not at all. Micaiah was not stupid; on the contrary, he was a faithful prophet of God. He had determined not to please man, only to be faithful to God. He affirmed, "As the Lord lives, what the Lord says to me, that I will speak."

Micaiah knowingly took the risk of inciting Ahab's wrath when he decided to please the Lord. The value of such a person is more than four hundred prophets put together. Our Chinese sage has said, "A thousand answers of assent in response to a call are not equal to the honest criticism of a scholar." This axiom could appropriately be applied to Micaiah and the four hundred prophets.

The messenger sent by Ahab to call Micaiah was truly diplomatic.

The Missing Voice

He did not not wish to see Micaiah entrapped so he briefed him about the situation ahead of time, advising him, "The words of the prophets are uniformly favorable to the king. So please let your word be like the word of one of them, and speak favorably." Even from these few words we can assume that Micaiah often spoke independently on matters when consulted by the king and that this was well known by the people of his kingdom. The messenger, therefore, surmised that Micaiah would follow his pattern and probably speak negatively. But because he esteemed this loyal prophet, he tried his best to warn him not to be stubborn and invite calamity. His concern may not have been from God but of the flesh; and this kind of good intention could have ruined the brave prophet. Fortunately he had already prepared his counsel and so he assured the messenger that he would speak only what God wanted him to speak.

Obviously, to be a prophet of God one must clearly know God's commission and will, and never be taken in, or easily accept the advice of others. After one clearly sees the will of God, one should carry it out no matter what the consequences, saying what God wants said, doing what God wants done. Otherwise, one is not qualified to be a prophet of God.

In this record there is one thing that may cause us to wonder. The first time Micaiah came before Ahab and was asked whether the king should go to Ramoth-gilead to battle, why did he echo the advice of the four hundred prophets: "Go up and succeed, and the Lord will give it into the hand of the king"? Did he suddenly give in and follow the faulty advice of the messenger? If so, fortunately this weakness lasted only for a moment and he soon regained his usual boldness and spoke what God wanted him to speak. But it may be just as likely that he was speaking the words in a flippant manner or with a sarcastic tone, so that they obviously rang false. In any case, the result was the same—it drew out of Ahab the question, "How many times must I adjure you to speak to me nothing but the truth in the name of the Lord?" Ahab just couldn't believe that his favorable words were the truth this time and challenged him. Then Micaiah spoke up as usual with a pessimistic prophecy.

"I saw all Israel scattered on the mountains, like sheep which have no shepherd. And the Lord said, 'These have no master. Let each of them return to his house in peace.' "

These few words clearly implied that the king of Israel would die and the people would become scattered like sheep without a shepherd. Micaiah continued to speak out what he knew to be true. He related that he had seen the Lord sitting on His throne and inquiring of the hosts of heaven who would entice Ahab to go up and fall at Ramoth-gilead. Finally a spirit came forward and said that he would go out and be a deceiving spirit in the mouth of all Ahab's prophets. The Lord then allowed him to go, and he did what was declared, so that the four hundred prophets all spoke the same lie. This was to result in Ahab being enticed into battle, to be killed at Ramoth-gilead.

Who was this "deceiving spirit"? We may compare this episode with the words of Jesus to gain some insight. "You are of your father the devil, and you want to do the desires of your father. He was a murderer from the beginning, and does not stand in the truth, because there is no truth in him. Whenever he speaks a lie, he speaks from his own nature; for he is a liar, and the father of lies."[1]

There was another scene narrated in the book of Job. "Now there was a day when the sons of God came to present themselves before the Lord, and Satan also came among them."[2] This clear record confirms the fact that the devil and the heavenly host served before the Lord. What Micaiah saw must have been a similar scene.

Another question is raised: Assuming that at least some of those four hundred men were actually prophets, how could the devil enter into all of their mouths to speak lies? Logically, only the spirit of God should be able to speak through the mouth of a prophet. Surely the spirit of the devil cannot—dare not—enter into a prophet's mouth! It is said, "The false cannot invade the true." Yes, prophets are supposed to be God's servants, so naturally we expect them to be upright. How could an evil spirit possess them?

If prophets indeed fear God and are faithful to Him, an evil spirit will never take them over. But those four hundred prophets had already shown that they did not fear God, nor were they faithful to God. All they could do was please Ahab. Therefore, it seems obvious that the Spirit of God had already departed from them. They were cast aside by God. Now they were on the same level as ordinary people. For them to have the spirit of the devil enter their mouths is not surprising.

The Missing Voice   39

Some might defend the four hundred prophets, saying, "How do you know that they didn't fear God nor were faithful to God, and that the Spirit of God had already left them?" I do not make such a statement without good reason. Notice first what kind of a man Ahab was. An extremely wicked person before God, he followed his wife Jezebel in Baal worship and built a temple and altar for Baal. The Bible states: "Ahab did evil in the sight of the Lord more than all who were before him."[3] He had permitted his wife to kill many of the prophets of the Lord. Some who had survived that persecution were, perhaps, numbered among the four hundred now before him.[4] He also did a most despicable deed by coveting Naboth's vineyard and permitting his wife to bear false witness in order to kill Naboth and seize his vineyard. Confronting such an extremely immoral king, any true prophet could not help but warn him to turn from his wicked ways.

Elijah, the prophet of God, when he saw Ahab, rebuked and advised him; therefore Ahab had hated him intensely. He called him "my enemy."[5] Micaiah too was God's prophet, and whenever he saw Ahab he took the opportunity to pronounce God's judgment even though this incited Ahab's hatred. But what was the case with these four hundred prophets?

Notice that Ahab summoned all except Micaiah. This plainly shows that these four hundred usually spoke whatever Ahab wanted to hear, and if he wanted to be blessed in his wicked ways, they went ahead and blessed him. If these people had not been prophets, their sin would not have been as serious. Nor should we conclude that these men were prophets of Baal; they were recognized as prophets of the Lord. But they were unfaithful. They didn't rebuke and admonish that extremely vicious king; instead they flattered and sought to please him, so that Ahab became even more daring as he continued in his evil ways.

These prophets had no right, really, to continue to be called prophets. More accurately, they ought to have been labeled as enemies of God. Their condition had become so corrupt that they were no longer righteous. Obviously we can conclude that the Spirit of God had left them. They had been cast away by the Lord. Of course Satan could now do with them whatever he wished and use them to his own ends. The spirit of lying could naturally enter their mouths at Satan's will, and they became the means of tempting Ahab to be killed at Ramoth-gilead. Faithful prophets like Elijah and Micaiah could not be touched by this evil spirit. Not only could such a spirit not enter their mouths, it would not even dare to come close to them. Because of this, Micaiah could clearly see what these prophets could not see and speak accurate words from God that these prophets could not speak.

This is a lamentable episode! The Israelites were God's chosen people. When their king led them into sin, the four hundred prophets who should have raised up a standard against the evil all fell short of their task by not daring to faithfully proclaim God's word or rebuke the sin of the king. All they could do was to utter praising, soothing, pleasant words which were untrue. That was the way for them to avoid Ahab's persecution and at the same time attract benefits from Ahab. If there had been no Elijah and Micaiah, the two courageous, faithful prophets commissioned to convey God's words, one might suspect that the Lord had entirely abandoned His people, the Israelites.

May God be praised! In any generation God has His own witnesses and raises up His prophets! He anoints them with His Spirit and fills them with strength and courage from above, to be His mouthpieces to proclaim His will. At the same time, He provides an opportunity for men to repent. If people are willing to hear their words and warnings they can then "rein in the horse from going over the cliff lest they fall to their death."

Just imagine what would have happened if Ahab had accepted Micaiah's warning and not only refrained from sending his army into battle at Ramoth-gilead but had fallen on his face before the Lord, weeping, confessing, and departing from his wicked ways. Would not this great calamity have been averted? If Ahab had been perceptive, he could have known that Micaiah was not to be hated but was actually his benefactor. Alas! He not only rejected the word of Micaiah, he decided to punish him, commanding, "Put this man in prison, and feed him sparingly with bread and water until I return safely."[6] Stubborn and obstinate to such a degree, how could the king escape the wrath of God?

There is another person here whom we should notice—Zedekiah

the son of Chenaanah. He was one of the four hundred prophets. Before Micaiah came on the scene he had made for himself two horns of iron. These he displayed before Ahab, saying, "Thus says the Lord, 'With these you shall gore the Syrians until they be consumed.'" This must have made Ahab very happy, because he thought that when the army attacked this time they would not merely regain a city that had been lost but would also destroy the Syrians utterly. What an unexpected bonus! He was probably ready to burst with joy. But he didn't realize that the one who spoke so optimistically before him was actually sending him to his death. Because he believed this false word, he would definitely not draw back. He would indeed be killed in the battle of Ramoth-gilead. To be pleased with one who is sending you to death while hating the one who could save you from death—does that not make Ahab an utterly foolish man?

There was not only that one Ahab. Throughout history, have not many been just like Ahab? The majority of people are happy to hear soothing words but abhor unpleasant words; they are delighted with flattering words but despise words of advice and rebuke. Cunning men understand psychology and use it to their own ends, always seeking to please. They use words that eulogize—praising and well-wishing words—so that those who listen may swell with joy. Through such flattery they expect to gain something for themselves. Those who hear will not notice their shortcomings or sense danger any more; but because they become ever more proud and arrogant, doing as they wish, they eventually fall into great calamity.

Were we a little wiser, we would immediately back off from people who speak such comfortable words; at the same time we would draw closer to those who dare to rebuke us, admonish us, and speak true words which may not be pleasing to listen to. Only such people can benefit us, lead us to repent and turn to God, thus enabling us to escape danger and calamity. Too bad that such people are so rare in the world. I will say that such people are even rarer in the church. They are scarce among believers and scarcer still among Christian leaders. There were four hundred prophets who flattered Ahab but only one prophet who did not value his own welfare, who did not care that others slandered him, because he was determined simply to be faithful to God. The situation in the nation of Israel in those days is parallel to that in the church of God today.

The prophet who was faithful to God then received a slap in the face from Zedekiah. Notice that the man who struck Micaiah was not one of Ahab's officials but actually a fellow prophet. Since Zedekiah was a prophet too, why should he want to strike one of his own? Zedekiah struck him *because* he was a prophet. If he himself had not been a prophet, he might not have dared to strike him. But what actually was his motive?

Zedekiah and the rest of the prophets had all declared that Ahab would win in the battle, but Micaiah maintained that Ahab would die in battle. If what Zedekiah said was true, then what Micaiah said had to be false. But if Micaiah's word was right, then Zedekiah's had to be wrong. If Zedekiah had not responded in some way to Micaiah, he would have admitted that Micaiah's words were accurate, at the same time confessing himself to be controlled by the spirit of lying. If for no other reason, he had to strike Micaiah to make a show of maintaining his own integrity. By striking Micaiah he asserted before all, "Micaiah has spoken irresponsibly and has slandered all the prophets. He should be struck." Such action would declare that it was not the four hundred prophets who were wrong, but Micaiah.

The officials of Ahab had nothing to gain or lose, so not one among them rose up to strike Micaiah. But because these two prophets were diametrically opposed in their proclamations, there was a natural clash between them. This caused Zedekiah to lash out and strike Micaiah.

That sort of thing happens all the time. The faithful prophets of God are hated and persecuted wherever they are. But there are two kinds of people who hate and persecute them the most. There are those who are being rebuked and warned but who refuse to repent. And there are those who are unfaithful in preaching God's Word but who habitually flatter and praise men.

To be a faithful prophet of God is not an easy task. Such a person will inevitably be opposed and hated by many. But they are indeed the most blessed ones because they will be greatly rewarded by God. The prophets who habitually flatter and speak well in front of men will not be hated and attacked by them. They are enthusiastically praised and welcomed. But they will inevitably meet calamity before God. That will be their greatest loss. Our Lord clearly described the end

The Missing Voice

of these two kinds of prophets: "Blessed are you when men hate you, and ostracize you, and heap insults upon you, and spurn your name as evil, for the sake of the Son of Man. Be glad in that day, and leap for joy, for behold, your reward is great in heaven; for in the same way their fathers used to treat the prophets.... Woe to you when all men speak well of you, for in the same way their fathers used to treat the false prophets."[7]

- - - - - - -

Background verses used in the above text:

[1] John 8:44
[2] Job 1:6; 2:1
[3] 1 Kings 16:30-33
[4] 1 Kings 18:4
[5] 1 Kings 21:20
[6] 1 Kings 22:26,27
[7] Luke 6:22,23,26

五　看那神的僕人

5
Look at God's Servant

> *Let the elders who rule well be considered worthy of double honor, especially those who work hard at preaching and teaching* —1 Timothy 5:17.

A person who works for God has no authority and power in and of himself. But he can earn the respect of people he ministers to so that they will heed his message, love him and trust him. One reason is that God is using him and has bestowed spiritual authority on him. God will, at the same time, move some believers to respect and love him from their hearts and to listen to his message. Another reason is because he himself has a high moral character, so that people of God recognize God's holiness and righteousness within and through him. As a result, they cannot help honoring him and his message from the depths of their hearts.

These two reasons are actually linked together. When God greatly uses a man, that man will surely live a life of holiness and magnanimity. And only if he is living such a life will God greatly use him. These two have mutual cause and effect.

The apostle Paul was a man greatly used by God and also respected and loved by others. The Galatian church received him ". . .as an angel of God, as Christ Jesus Himself. . . ,"[1] and they were willing to pluck out their eyes and give them to Paul if necessary. When he was in Thessalonica, the church in Philippi ". . .sent a gift more than once for my needs."[2] When he said farewell to the elders of Ephesus at Miletus and prayed with them, they "began to weep aloud and embraced Paul, and repeatedly kissed him, . . .accompanying him to the ship."[3] The Bible also records an episode in Caesarea when the believers wept and begged Paul not to proceed into danger awaiting him at Jerusalem.[4] Certainly these records are proof enough that at that time the believers who knew Paul well, loved him, respected him, and were concerned about him.

That Paul was greatly used by God and loved and respected by believers was not by accident. His godly life was the basis for the Lord greatly using him and, consequently, the believers loving him. When he addressed the believers in Thessalonica, he said, "You are witnesses, and so is God, how *devoutly* and *uprightly* and *blamelessly* we behaved toward you believers."[5]

These three simple words, "devoutly and uprightly and blamelessly," are endued with much meaning. I think they might imply that Paul was not careless about money, not greedy, and in his relationships with the opposite sex was clear cut and of pure conduct. He displayed no prejudice when living among those of another culture, nor did he hold back any of his message for fear of giving offense to men. He was responsible in what he said, kept the trust of others, and was never jealous but esteemed others better than himself. He did not hate anyone who offended him, did not easily criticize or judge others, and did not show off or boast about himself. He observed rules, obeyed laws, respected the elderly, loved children, respected the property of others, and was concerned about the joy and sorrow of neighbors. He did not easily express anger, nor abruptly speak out; he was humble and kind, meek and approachable. He hated evil, loved that which was good, and was neither careless nor negligent in the smallest matters. I believe we can surely read all the above details of his lifestyle into those three simple but all-encompassing terms describing Paul's character.

Some might ask, "Is Paul's assessment of his own character actually true? Since people sometimes like to boast about themselves, would Paul be any exception?"

My answer is, Paul's self-evaluation is without exaggeration because he boldly called on two witnesses to attest it. One of them was the believers who were reading his epistle: "You are my witnesses." The second one was God Himself: "God is my witness." How valid are these two witnesses! Paul would not dare to face the believers in Thessalonica and invite them to witness that he was devout, upright and blameless if it were not true. This would seem to be adequate already to prove that his claims were one hundred percent true. Otherwise he would not have such audacity to state that. He knew for sure that they couldn't find any fault or evil doings in him, so he dared to call on their witness.

The second witness was God. He not only dared to invite the believers to be his witness, but he dared to directly invoke the almighty and all-knowing God too as witness. We may conclude that even in his solitary life, when no one was with him, he must have been just as devout, upright and blameless as in public. If it were not so, he would not have dared to invoke God as his witness. He may have appeared blameless before men but it would not necessarily follow for a man to be blameless before God. But if one were blameless before God, he would surely be blameless before men. Now Paul was such before both God and men. He didn't hesitate for a moment to call upon these two witnesses. Such a worker for God could not help but have authority and power.

Yes, workers for God need gifts and talents, but more important than gifts, they need high moral character. For if one is without gifts to work for God, the worst that could happen would only be that there might not be much in the way of accomplishment in the eyes of men. If he is a man of high moral principle he will never disgrace God and harm people because of his lack of gifts. If a person has many gifts, yet is without high moral character, at a certain point in time he might be accomplishing much work. . . but after a while, what he did would be ruined by his own wicked deeds. God would be greatly disgraced and many people would certainly be harmed by him. I'm sure we have all heard about such cases. What are workers for God in the churches today usually seeking after? It is not necessary to consider those preachers who really do not have faith and hence no spiritual life. Let us rather take a look at those who *do* have real faith and life and are willing to serve God. The majority of them pay much attention to the need for entering seminaries, searching the Scripture, understanding the truth, learning homiletics, pastoral theology, church history, Palestinian geography, studying comparative religions, the Hebrew and Greek languages, and preparing hundreds of sermons. Some seem to think that by such preparation they may become honorable instruments in God's hands and faithful servants in the household of God. As for spiritual authority and holy living, however, these do not seem to carry so much weight in their esteem. How can God greatly use such persons and how can they have spiritual effectiveness in the church?

In 1 Timothy 3:2-12, the Bible clearly states what workers of God should be like. The two kinds of positions set forth for the church—bishops and deacons—have high qualifications. Among the many mentioned, only two are concerned with the gifts and the work and the rest are all concerned with high character and moral conduct. The function of the church is simply to obey God's command in this regard, to pay attention to what God wants us to pay attention to. We must seek for such workers as God wants us to have. In so doing, we will be blessed by God and will not fail to see the glory of God.

Looking at the lives of the majority of church leaders surely causes us to weep. . . but without tears. Lying, deceiving, indulging in evil practices, embezzlement, subversion, pushing others aside to exalt themselves, quarreling, envying, hating, slandering, flattering others, being greedy, seeking fame, engaging in adulterous acts, yielding to sensual pleasures—with shame we must admit that all such sins become commonplace practice among them. If leaders of the church indulge in such, how can we expect believers in general to be any better? If the church has degenerated to such corruption and darkness, how can God's name not be blasphemed by outsiders? This cannot help but cause immature and weak believers to stumble and fall. Such leaders as above are utterly useless before God and will surely be cast out by God. For His own great name's sake, God will prepare vessels for Himself to use. Notice how He cast aside Saul in ancient times and raised up David. Today He will likewise raise up a people after His own heart. These people may be rich in education, in gifts surpassing others, or, on the other hand, they may not have any special talents. But they will have a godly life and superior bearing. Because they have this essential character that God counts of most value, He can then greatly use them and manifest His power and glory through them. Because they have the kind of character that people respect most, they will be honored and loved by those to whom they minister, be trusted by them, and their message obeyed. Consequently they will become most honored and great, having spiritual authority. Then they can say what Paul said by inviting the same witnesses as Paul did—the believers who know them and God who discerns the hearts of men. God will also work through them as He did through Paul. Finally, when Christ appears, they will be rewarded as Paul was. How glorious and joyful that will be!

- - - - - - -

Background verses used in the above text:
[1] Galatians 4:14, 15
[2] Philippians 4:16
[3] Acts 20:36-38
[4] Acts 21:10-14
[5] 1 Thessalonians 2:10

六　　　　　　　　　錦繡枕頭

6
Success & Embroidered Pillows

> *"His master said to him, 'Well done, good and faithful slave; you were faithful with a few things, I will put you in charge of many things, enter into the joy of your master'"* —Matthew 25:21.

On the evening before His arrest, the Lord Jesus prayed to His Father, "I have glorified Thee on the earth, having accomplished the work which Thou hast given Me to do."[1] He had lived on this earth for scarcely thirty-three years, a carpenter by trade. As an itinerant teacher His travels had been limited to the vicinity of Galilee and Judea. He had performed various miracles, healed many sick persons, and preached to great crowds. But while doing so He made numerous enemies and aroused the strong opposition of many.

Early in His ministry He chose twelve of His disciples and named them as apostles. Although they were comparatively few, yet they selfishly fought over who would be the greatest in His kingdom. Among these dozen followers there was one who ultimately conceived in his heart to sell his Lord to wicked men for a mere thirty pieces of silver. Jesus realized that after a few more hours He would be arrested, arraigned and sentenced to death. The next day He would be nailed to the cross and His earthly life would be at an end. From every outward appearance, His life had accomplished little except defeat, suffering and shame.

Popular expectations for the Jewish Messiah were that He would be a glorious, powerful ruler who would astound the whole world, defeating His foes and restoring the Kingdom of Israel. When Jesus began His preaching and healing ministry, many set that kind of hope on Him. So far He had not lived up to their expectations and they could not help but be greatly disappointed in Him. Even His own cousin, John, the witness, who baptized Him, began to have his doubts. He sent two of his own disciples from prison to check out the truth. "Are You the Coming One, or shall we look for someone else?"[2] We must remember that after Jesus fed the five thousand people on the hillside by the Sea of Galilee, the Jews had moved in eagerly to crown Him king. He rejected their overtures and retreated into the mountains to pray. He abandoned this excellent chance of becoming great in the eyes of men.[3]

After Jesus' crucifixion His disciples fell into the depths of despondency, as we can clearly see from the mood of the two disciples on their way to Emmaus. When Jesus appeared and questioned them on the road about their discussion, "...they stood still, looking sad."[4] The one called Cleophas informed the stranger of their dashed hopes about "Jesus the Nazarene, who was a prophet mighty in deed and word. But we were hoping that it was He who was going to redeem Israel."[5] What a letdown! Jesus' death had dealt an overwhelming blow of despair to the disciples. They felt forced to consider their Lord as a defeated one, a view shared by many others.

But Jesus Himself did not view His life in that light. Just before His suffering He evaluated His life before His Heavenly Father in terms of having glorified God and accomplished God's goals. From the human perspective, success is measured by the achievement of many great enterprises. Jesus measured His life by the accomplish-

Success & Embroidered Pillows 53

ment of the task God had committed to Him, and He judged that it was a success. He had lived on earth for only a few years and had not accomplished outwardly great things, but He had truly invested His whole life to glorify God and do what God expected of Him. Others despised Him, thought Him different and peculiar, even insane; certainly He had never gained the approval of the establishment. He looked like a failure. But in the eyes of God He had done God's task. In the eyes of people, the Jesus hanging on the cross was a defeated Jesus; but in the eyes of God He was a successful Jesus. Jesus understood the heart of God: He knew God's will, and that is why He could make such a declaration in prayer before His Father.

Was Jesus really successful? Yes, truly yes! But what might be the proof of it? Look at the empty tomb and the napkin and the linen laid aside there. Hear what the two angels in shining garments declared: "Why do you seek the living One among the dead? He is not here, but He has risen...."[6] Look at the record of His resurrection, how He appeared several times to His disciples. Heed the importance of His words to His disciples after His resurrection: "All authority has been given to Me in heaven and on earth."[7] Again, mark the glorious fact that Luke records: "And after He had said these things, He was lifted up while they were looking on, and a cloud received Him out of their sight."[8] If He had not been successful, He would not have had this glorious resurrection and ascension. If He had not been successful, God would not have given Him all power in heaven and on earth. If He had not been successful, He would not have been received up to sit at the right hand of God. This series of glorious facts is in itself enough to prove that He had indeed been the greatest success.

Beyond these attesting events, the apostle Paul wrote that Jesus humbled Himself by coming to the earth and becoming man, subject to human limitations.[9] But Luke recorded for our knowledge an even greater, more glorious fact: that the same Jesus who ascended into heaven would one day return in like manner.[10] At that time He shall come in the clouds and receive us unto Himself.[11] Without question He had been despised and falsely charged, suffering many insults...yet never before had one been as greatly successful as He.

Today, we who believe in Him should desire the same kind of success as Jesus had. We should pursue it earnestly. It is not the success of accomplishing great and splendid enterprises, but of glorifying God on earth and accomplishing what God has committed to us. Some Christians excel in social relationships: flattering people, manipulating others psychologically, being men-pleasers, crafty, putting on a mask, puffing up themselves, propagandizing their efforts. By these means they succeed in climbing high in society or within the church. They are esteemed by many as having accomplished great things in the world—many splendid achievements. But they have never glorified God nor fulfilled what He has committed to them. In the eyes of men such people are successful; but before God they are failures.

On the other hand, there are other Christians just like their Lord, neither striving nor making noise. No one has heard their voice on the street. Also like their Lord, they have been despised, rejected, made sorrowful and full of grief. But they have actually lived a superior life by glorifying God and trying their best to fulfill what God has committed to them. They have received no one's praises but God's. They attracted little glory on this earth; but they will receive the greatest glory when Christ comes into His kingdom.

The popular view is that to be a success one must possess superior talents. Otherwise, how can one possibly overcome the competition? If this were so, ordinary Christians would have no hope of attaining success. But no Christian should consider himself ordinary and unable to attain success in the eyes of God. Today those who measure themselves as successful ridicule dedicated Christians as imbeciles, foolish, useless and stupid; but should they enter the kingdom of Christ they will come to realize that the real imbeciles, foolish, useless and stupid persons were none other than themselves. We don't need to envy those seemingly successful persons. We should not bemoan the fact that we do not have superior talents or special luck. Nor should we try to imitate the "success" of others.

Yes, every Christian can become a success in the eyes of God. The time we are given and the work that is set before us are ordained by God, and *these* are the opportunities of our success. Even a sweaty farmer, a laborer working all the day, a housewife exercising her chores, an illiterate villager—each needs only to lead a devout life in the will of God in order to fulfill what God has destined him to do. Such are without question *successful in God's sight.* God wants no outward show but rather inward reality; not achievement but faithfulness.

So then, can the *talented* Christian also become a success in God's sight? Certainly he can. With talents he can go on to accomplish greater spiritual achievements. But he must first come humbly before God, placing his trust wholeheartedly in God, and must not rely on his own understanding or talents. He must not consider himself wise, but fear the Lord and depart from evil. He must purge from his heart any attitude of sophistication and pride; lay aside all craftiness and high-mindedness. He must not masquerade as what he is not. He should not use flattery, become a man-pleaser, take advantage of others, or seek self-exaltation. Such Christians need to shun the glory of man but seek the glory of God. They must renounce their wild ambitions, selfish goals and worldly methods. They must seek to glorify God in all things so that others may be benefited. They must walk the path which Jesus walked: "humbling Himself, obedient unto death." If very gifted Christians are faithful to God, they will be all the more successful indeed. But people with many gifts and talents are seldom willing to give up human glory and solely seek glory from God. How pitiful that is!

How few are the people in churches today who are seeking success in God's sight! Is that surprising? We don't have to look far to see some zealous, active leaders who are putting on airs in the church today. Aren't they paying more attention to the success of their own enterprises than to their inward piety and devotion? They concentrate on holding large meetings, erecting huge church buildings, training flashy choirs, organizing big gospel teams, reporting staggering statistics, blowing their own horns, receiving great numbers of church members. The emphasis in all these endeavors is on "big." But in the final analysis, these works show pitifully little of those things which God values most.

Of course we do not oppose or belittle the believers who hold large meetings, build huge churches, organize large gospel teams. They are laboring for the Lord. But we shouldn't give all of our attention to these and neglect God's imperatives upon us to be faithful, obedient and devout servants. If we first have these most precious attributes, the Spirit of God will work mightily within us and then there will naturally flow from our ministries many great works, great results and true success. That is a higher level of achievement; that is what God expects of us. Our Lord did say that we would do greater works than even He did because He was going to His Father.[12] But if we do not pay attention to that which God wants—our inward success—but spend all our time on outward greatness in our lives and work, we will become like embroidered pillows: the outward appearance is very beautiful while the interior is filled with worthless stuffing.

Take a look at some of the "zealous Christian leaders" in the church today, at the lives of some so-called evangelists and revivalists. How pitiful they are! Their work appears to be very great; their fame has spread far and wide. Everywhere their reports and testimonies are really moving. But if we carefully watch their lives, we will discover their inward greediness, ambition for fame, hypocrisy, envy and strife, quarrelsomeness, jealousy, soiled hearts and unholy intentions. What they preach is indeed pure, but their lives are not pure. They do not have those very choice things within themselves, so of course they cannot effectively communicate and teach others to seek the best things. They put all their efforts into encouraging their congregations to work hard for the Lord and to accomplish outwardly great things. The only thing the world pays attention to today is the big, but not necessarily the genuine; quantity rather than quality; outward achievement but not inward contentment. Unfortunately this applies to Christians as well. Even to the actively serving ones, even to zealous Christian leaders—what a sorrowful situation!

But no matter how people insist on exalting the ostentatious, God persists in paying attention to the genuine. People esteem quantity; God values quality. People admire what they can see; God desires inward reality. If we are not aiming to please God, we can get away with this low view and still receive the world's commendation—but we do not receive the commendation of God. If we *do* want to please God, then we must pay attention to what *He* esteems. Otherwise, whatever we accomplish that looks like great success in the eyes of men is still a failure in God's sight. Even the most successful person in the esteem of men may actually be the greatest failure in God's sight.

I have learned a most interesting lesson from viewing certain storefronts in the marketplace in Peking. Viewed from the front, they appear to be two stories: below, attractive merchandise is displayed in the showcases; above, the windows are decorated with curtains. These apparently two-story buildings look beautiful and are attractively painted. One concludes that they must be large department stores. But when you enter the door, you discover that the goods in the store are not as high quality and abundant as you expected. The building is tiny and cramped and the goods are sparse. You are amazed that the inside of the store is far different from the outside. When you back away from the building and take another careful look, you discover that the building is not even a two-story building but has a high front-wall built along the street. On the upper part of the wall what appeared to be windows actually are only decorated windowpanes hung with curtains! From the front one cannot tell that they are false. The proprietor did this to attract people—to make them think that his store is large and his merchandise plentiful and of good quality.

There are other stores too, which, although they do not have false windows, do have a separate wall erected in front of the building, painted with beautiful scenery and impressive characters so that the passerby will think that the stores are high class.

Many Christians and Christian leaders have a lifestyle that is just like those storefronts—the outside is big and beautiful but the inside is small and debased. The outside is impressive, and at first appearance men do not notice the illusion. But God can certainly search out the real. People, too, will eventually see through such a facade. They who seek outward glory will end up with shame; the crafty will be exposed as fools. How tragic!

Paul draws an illustration concerning success in God's sight and in the eyes of men. Two kinds of works are contrasted, being pictured as materials which either can withstand burning fire or are consumed. "Each man's work will become evident; for the day will show it," he declares.[13] The gold, silver and precious stones refer to quality work that can withstand the test of fire; one needs to pay much money and expend great effort to get just a small amount of these valuable commodities. The latter three, the wood, hay and stubble, one need only pay a small sum and expend less effort to obtain—but they cannot stand the test of fire. They will turn to ashes.

In God's sight, real success is to have one's work valued as gold, silver and precious stones. When a person is forced to go through much labor or sorrow, with patience and faithfulness, the result does not seem to be much but those qualities are real, eternal, and valuable in God's sight. Human success is like the works of wood, hay and stubble. Such works take little exertion or faithfulness. A little "blowing" from the outside and a little bustling around will serve to give the appearance of a magnificent outward result.

Yes, many may repent and believe as a result of big meetings—many may even join the church—but all these seemingly magnificent results can be just trifling and temporary, without genuine value in God's sight.

Oh, how many zealous Christians' works are like wood, hay and stubble! How many zealous Christian leaders' works are also like these perishable things! But they are appreciated and applauded by the crowd. That is a sorrowful thing. We should quickly awaken, we should quickly repent. Let us not long for and pursue human success. Let us seek success in God's sight with an undivided mind, so that at the end of our life's journey, without the slightest doubt or regret, we too may report to God as Jesus did, "I have accomplished what Thou hast committed to me."

- - - - - - -

Background verses used in the above text:

1. John 17:4
2. Matthew 11:2,3
3. John 6:15
4. Luke 24:17
5. Luke 24:19-21
6. Luke 24:5,6
7. Matthew 28:18
8. Acts 1:9
9. Philippians 2:5-11
10. Acts 1:11
11. 1 Thessalonians 4:16,17
12. John 14:12
13. 1 Corinthians 3:10-15

七

一個投機的少年

7
A Young Opportunist

Who may ascend into the hill of the Lord? And who may stand in His holy place? He who...has not lifted up his soul to falsehood, and has not sworn deceitfully —Psalm 24:3,4.

A certain young Amalekite whose story is recorded in the Old Testament must have been a very ambitious character. As he looked over the battlefield on Mount Gilboa he spotted the body of Saul, the king; so he removed the royal crown and bracelet from it and decided to deliver them to David with the hope of receiving his favor and a reward. To go along with this, he made up a story about having killed Saul at Saul's request because he was mortally wounded and begging to be put out of his agony.[1] The true facts were not so, as Saul had actually committed suicide by falling on his own sword after the battle went disastrously against Israel.[2] If the young man had truthfully stated what had happened to the king when he brought his crown and bracelet to David, he might have been rewarded for having kept Saul's possessions from falling into the hands of the victorious Philistines. Unfortunately, his ambition backfired and resulted in his own hurt. He must have been unaware of the actual relationship between David and Saul and assumed that since David had been pursued by Saul, he would be quite happy that Saul was dead.

In any case, the young man did not think that he was taking much of a chance with his fabricated story because, whatever the consequences, it could only come out to his credit. If David was glad to hear that Saul had been killed, he would surely honor the messenger with a reward. Should David not be happy about Saul's death, he still would not appear guilty of any wrongdoing—because it was Saul himself who requested him to finish him off. His lie was well thought through, and he gambled on it succeeding. If perchance it should fail, he could not conceive that he would be losing anything for trying. It was because he felt so confident that he resolutely decided to capitalize on this grand opportunity.

The young man never imagined that David might rebuke him for "destroying the Lord's anointed." Doubtless, when he began to realize that his falsehood was bringing him no benefit but rather might cause him personal suffering, he regretted his lie. But it was too late then to remedy the wrong he had done, and he could no longer have won the confidence of David. So with fear and trembling he awaited David's sentence. Then he heard the dread command of David, "Go, cut him down."[3] and he was struck dead.

This young man was actually quite crafty. Other people might have taken the crown and bracelet from Saul's body and hidden them, waiting for an opportunity to sell them. But he probably calculated that those items could be worn by no one except the king and were certainly recognizable, so that no one would dare to either buy or wear them. If he had hidden the items, not only would it have been useless but he would have risked discovery and further trouble. He should have figured that the safest and most beneficial way was simply to bring them to David with the factual story. If he had done that, and only that, he would probably have been rewarded. It is too bad that his greedy heart incited him to try for a greater gain. He used

A Young Opportunist

his craftiness to try to deceive David. The result? The reward he expected was not forthcoming; instead, his own life was taken. "The ambitious man may find that his own ambition brings harm to himself" might be an appropriate comment.

It is true that it is mostly the ambitious people of this world who tell such grand lies. Usually they think through very methodically how they will do things, weighing all aspects of the matter, until they are sure that, whatever happens, they have nothing to lose. They forget there is a God in heaven who hates lies and treacherous schemes. They fail to heed His warnings: "Truthful lips will be established forever, but a lying tongue is only for a moment," and "Lying lips are an abomination to the Lord, but those who deal faithfully are His delight."[4] But no matter how thoroughly a person lies, no matter how people fail to see through the deception, God cannot be deceived. He sees all things and all men. However secret a man's scheme, God can find it out. He can demolish our best scheme with His little finger.

Many look at honest people as being rather foolish and impractical, but they fail to take into account that because of their honest character they are pleasing to God. Actually, honesty is the most important virtue of all. Since God is pleased with such persons, surely He will bless them. Something that looks like an obvious danger can, in fact, be safe; a "sure loss" can change into a profitable matter. To seek to please men does not compare with pleasing God; to seek man's help is not comparable to seeking God's help. An honest man may appear weak and naive before men, seemingly sure to suffer loss, but before God he is acceptable, receiving much gain and blessing. A crafty man may be acclaimed by men and counted as a genius, but before God he will invite curses and suffer loss. The Bible clearly shows us God's evaluation of the honesty and dishonesty of men.

Many people in the world are just like this young Amalekite. They take every chance they can get to pursue fame and seek their own gain. They resort to dubious practices to further their own interests; they lie and deceive others. They may use psychology on people to gain their favor. They fully attend to every detail of matters to impress others with their high character. They think that their scheming is very secure: advance to attack, retreat to defend—that, however it may turn out, they are not risking their own loss or harm. They tailor their words to suit whoever they meet. They are skilled in being all things to all men, in the eyes of others. They may temporarily receive some profit and glory—that stimulates them to become more daring, fearless and quite elated, counting on everything going smoothly without a hitch. They do not realize that one day God's wrath will suddenly fall on them. Their schemes will inevitably be exposed, their lies revealed, until they find themselves down and out, regretting... but too late. They thought they were wiser than others; actually they were the most foolish of all.

From time immemorial, people have been lying and deceiving each other, causing all sorts of misfortune and calamities. Such examples from the past should be enough to warn people. Unfortunately, the majority of people see the facts but still don't take any warning. They somehow think that though others who have lied were exposed, surely they themselves will escape—even receive much gain. Others who play tricks might fail, but not themselves; no, they will succeed! Their sin has blinded their hearts so that they hear but do not understand, see but do not perceive. Consequently, one after the other they fall into the pit of calamity. Although there may be people around shouting to warn them, they cover their ears so as not to hear. What a sad plight!

We should hurriedly awaken. We know that God, who hates lies and deception, hates our sin, so we should abandon it promptly. "Deliver my soul, O Lord, from lying lips, from a deceitful tongue."[5] Knowing that God hates lies, we should determine that from this day on we will never engage in the slightest deceit or falsehood, never speak lies or stoop to tricks. Whenever we may be called on and wherever we are, we will be sincere of heart, speaking truthfully, doing honest things. It is far better that we should fail or be persecuted for being honest than that we should ever lie. We can rest assured that we will never invite God's wrath upon us through our honesty.

"Thou dost destroy those who speak falsehood; the Lord abhors the man of bloodshed and deceit."[6]

Background verses used in the above text:
1. 2 Samuel 1:1-16
2. 1 Samuel 31:1-6
3. 2 Samuel 1:15
4. Proverbs 12:19,22
5. Psalm 120:2
6. Psalm 5:6

八　不打折扣的信息

8
A Message Without Discount

> "*I did not shrink from declaring to you anything that was profitable,...the whole purpose of God*" —Acts 20:20a,27b.

The servant of God, the apostle Paul, declared to the elders of the church at Ephesus, "I did not shrink from declaring to you anything that was profitable,...the whole purpose of God."[1]

Every servant of God is responsible to do just that. It is the mandate he receives from God. God spoke to His servant Jeremiah: "All that I command you, you shall speak."[2] He instructed His servant Ezekiel: "But you shall speak My words unto them whether they listen or not...."[3] Just before Jesus ascended to heaven He charged His disciples to go to all nations, "...teaching them to observe all that I commanded you...."[4] Whether people heed or refuse to hear, the result is not in our hand. We are to go on teaching them to observe all that God has commanded. One has the option not to be a servant of God. But if one has taken that yoke upon himself, then it is imperative to be faithful to preach all of His words. Discounting not a word, we must preach God's truth to those in need.

God called Jeremiah, commissioning him to be His mouthpiece. What an honorable charge—to speak for God! God Himself seldom spoke directly to people. But He put His words into the mouths of His servants and told them to speak out for Him. As God's mouthpieces they were to say the words that God wanted to say to the people—no more, no less, sentence by sentence. To miss one sentence would be to miss God's commandment and to be unable to face God. That person would be an unqualified servant of God.

But to speak out all of the words of God is not easy. How can one who does not obey the message of God himself dare to speak out? If he does, his conscience accuses him. Furthermore, those who hear him could point their finger at him saying, "You yourself don't obey God's words; how dare you try to teach us to do so?" This is a strong reason why some of God's workers do not dare to speak the whole counsel of God. A person who has a certain sin himself does not dare rebuke that sin in others. How can he speak out boldly about a point of his own guilt?

The more one obeys the Word of God, the more one dares to speak out boldly. When such a man conveys God's message, he is not convicted by his own conscience and is not afraid of any reproof from others. When a servant of God is pleasing to God, God grants him special grace and power so that the more he speaks, the more power he has. His words become like thunderbolts to the ears of the people, powerful as a hammer. On the contrary, if a person does not obey God's will himself and is tainted with much sin, not only does his own conscience accuse him but those who hear him will mock him. God is not able to use such a person. How could God use a dirty channel as His mouthpiece?

Let us look at the lives of some of God's so-called servants in some places in the church today. We will see clearly that some are not eligible to be God's mouthpieces to convey His revealed truth. The lives of many are filthy and evil. Their thoughts and deeds are full of craftiness, hypocrisy, greed, lasciviousness, hatred, strife, lying, slander, viciousness, flattery and pride. We see them despising the poor, taking what does not belong to them, fighting for fame, not honoring their parents, not loving the brethren, betraying their friends and the Lord, breaking promises, disregarding loyalties, being selfish, ungrateful, etc. Unfortunately, any sin found in society at large can also be found among "God's servants." Let me ask, How can God use such people? How can people like that dare to speak God's message before men? Many who call themselves God's servants have themselves not yet repented nor believed in God and been born again. They are actually unsaved and unregenerate.

It is never easy for a true laborer of God to be a faithful person and obey God's Word. The majority of people are not willing to obey God's commands. I am not referring to idolaters and unbelievers but to those nominally called God's people. It is these who are seldom willing to be totally obedient to God's Word. When the servant of God declares warnings to the people of this world, rebuking them for sins, exhorting them to repent and turn to God, he naturally invites opposition. When he reproves the sins of the church and calls Christians to return to the right path, then also the truth cannot help but arouse ill feelings in those who hear. The flesh basically is not willing to obey God. If God's servants take a stand to be faithful and speak for God, they will inevitably meet antagonism at every turn. Surely if they accurately proclaim it, they will be disliked. But if they shrink back from speaking His full message, their own hearts will reprove them and they will feel inwardly uneasy. Truly this is a hard battle!

Jeremiah related his own experience of becoming a laughingstock before all when he proclaimed God's word.[5] He met with intense suffering and persecution simply because he was faithful to speak all that God had told him. Once, in a weak moment, he declared that he would not mention God any more nor speak any more in His name. But he could not desist. His heart felt as if God's word within him was like a burning fire shut up in his bones. He was weary of holding it in and could not suppress it. Though he was attacked and reproved from the outside, yet to quench God's word within him was harder to bear. "But the Lord is with me . . . ."[6] he affirmed, and continued courageously speaking the words of God.

Paul also fully experienced that to faithfully speak the message of God was not easy. That is why he taught his beloved son Timothy to be strong and pass on to other faithful men all that Paul had committed to him of God's word.[7] To be a soldier is unquestionably a hard and dangerous occupation. Speaking for God is like soldiering, very risky and perilous. On the other hand, if God's servants are motivated by desire for fame, money or earning a livelihood, theirs is a comparatively easy job. But let us face it, those who are faithful to God are usually unpopular. God's Word preached as such inevitably incites the anger of an audience, invites opposition and causes many to misunderstand. But because we have God's commission to proclaim it, we have no choice but to obey. There are great similarities between this situation and military action on the battlefield. No wonder Paul exhorted Timothy to be faithful, saying, "Suffer hardship with me, as a good soldier of Christ Jesus."[8]

Often in the church when God's servant mentions certain sins that people commit, as Christians in the congregation hear it they consider that he is personally attacking, exposing and insulting them. So they express their disagreement very strongly, even openly. I don't deny that there are some of God's servants who do use the occasion of preaching to attack those with whom they have some breach of relationship, but such people are not qualified to be called God's true servants. At the same time we also see some stubborn congregations who are repeatedly and justly warned and rebuked by God through His faithful servants. But not only do these people not feel ashamed, they are not at all contrite and rather turn their anger toward God's servant, counting him as their enemy. Certain of God's servants, for the sake of avoiding such opposition, take great pains not to aggravate the people as they preach. Therefore they do not dare to point out many of God's precious and important truths, nor dare to rebuke certain sins, but use much restraint in choosing the themes on which they preach. As a result, all that they can do is to selectively preach "safe sermons" unrelated to real faith and life and the needs of the people. Naturally they do not meet any opposition or make enemies. But they have totally lost their function before God and are in danger of being cast away from before Him.

Anyone who works for God should make an irrevocable decision whether he intends to please God or to please men. There is only

A Message Without Discount

one choice—a person cannot have it both ways. Paul not only understood this truth, he also made his own final decision and declared that he would not please men, for ". . . if I were still trying to please men, I would not be a bond-servant of Christ."[9] Ever since that time, all of God's true servants know they cannot escape opposition and persecution. Our Lord clearly taught us to expect it and that we are blessed when we receive it.[10] We should "rejoice and be glad" because our reward in heaven is great and we share this suffering with the prophets who were before us. At the same time, our Lord also told us that only the false prophets could please all men and they would be the ones who would be well spoken of.[11]

As for me, if I am not able to be a prophet who is faithful to God, I would rather not be a prophet at all. I never want to be the kind of prophet who provokes God's anger because he does not proclaim all that God wants, and brings harm to those who hear an incomplete message. In the end I would also damage myself.

But the servant of God who faithfully proclaims the revelation of God, though he will surely meet opposition and persecution, be reviled and defamed, does not need to fear. In times past, God promised to protect and shelter His servants; today He will do the same for those who faithfully proclaim His words. "Be not afraid of them, for I am with you to deliver you," declares the Lord. "They will fight against you, but they will not overcome you."[12] God assured Paul of the same thing.

Paul declared to the church that he was innocent of the blood of all of them because he did not shrink from declaring to them the whole counsel of God. Every worker of God should be able to say this in all good conscience and dare to proclaim it. Not only must we be able to say it, but we must follow it through to be qualified to be called worthy servants of God.

"But go on speaking and do not be silent, for I am with you."[13]

Background verses used in the above text:

[1] Acts 20:20,21,26,27
[2] Jeremiah 1:7,17
[3] Ezekiel 2:4-11
[4] Matthew 28:19,20
[5] Jeremiah 20:7-10
[6] Jeremiah 20:11
[7] 2 Timothy 2:1,2
[8] 2 Timothy 2:3
[9] Galatians 1:10-12
[10] Matthew 5:11,12
[11] Luke 6:26
[12] Jeremiah 1:8,19
[13] Acts 18:9,10

九

從世界所期望的

9

What to Expect from the World

"Blessed are those who have been persecuted for the sake of righteousness, for theirs is the kingdom of heaven" — Matthew 5:10.

Our Lord Jesus, without a doubt, was hated by the world. His disciples, He foretold, would receive similar treatment.[1] And what were the reasons for the world hating Jesus? Men love darkness—and Jesus was the Light of the world: He pointed out their evil and exposed their sins.[2] One way whereby Jesus shone brightly in the darkened world was His holy living, which automatically showed up the sins of men. Another way was through His spoken words—His teachings which exposed their evil ways. That is why He drew the hatred of many people. The world ridiculed Him, put Him to shame, hated Him, persecuted Him, and finally nailed Him to the cross.

Jesus instructed His disciples that if the world hated them, they must keep in mind that it hated Him first.[3] The Scriptures clearly state that the world hated our Lord. Naturally, then, it would hate His followers also. He wanted them to be forewarned that, since they followed Him, they could not avoid being hated by the world. Conversely, if one belongs to the world, he will be loved by it. This is very logical, because the world would not hate that which belongs to it. Then Jesus said, "...I chose you out of the world; therefore the world hates you."[4] He reminded them of what He had taught them previously: that no servant is greater than his master, so persecution was inevitable for them just as it was for Him.[5] More than that, the world not only hated Jesus but it hated the Father.[6] As the Son of God, Jesus was pleasing to God. So those who were loving the Father would also love Jesus. The Father, the Son, and His disciples; these three parties were inseparable, and what was the case for one was the case for the others.

In the high-priestly prayer of Jesus, in John chapter 17, He reiterated the fact that Christians are hated by the world because they don't belong to the world, just as their Lord is not of this world either.[7] The apostle John later told believers that their being hated by the world was but a natural consequence of their being different, and that they should not wonder at this.[8] Nor should *we* be surprised. The majority of people in this world are against God. In this anti-Christ generation, if Christians were *not* hated by the world, that *would be* surprising!

Maybe someone will ask, "Is it possible for Christians to avoid being hated by the world?" My answer is, Yes, it is possible. But such Christians must choose one of two roads. The first alternative: they must deny the name of Jesus Christ and be careful not to live the life of Christ. They must mingle with the world and do all the things which the world does. The second alternative is to openly confess that they are Christians...but then go hand in hand with those who are enemies of Christ and with them plan a strategy to persecute those who are faithfully following Christ. An example would be Judas, who collaborated with the enemy and led them to capture Jesus. "Christians" who take that road will not only not be hated by the world, they will surely be welcomed by the world. People will praise them, sympathize with them, become their friends, invite them to dinner and give them money to spend. Those who do as Judas did will receive the treatment Judas got—and they will end up like Judas too. If a Christian does not want to choose either of the two roads suggested above, but desires to follow Jesus closely, he will indeed be hated by the world just as his Master was hated. The more faithful he is to Jesus, the more he will be hated by the world. If he is totally obeying God's will like his Master, whatever happens to him in this world will be similar to what happened to the Lord.

From the time of the early church until now, Christians have been hated.[9] Whether they live in an idol-worshiping society or an atheistic society, or even in so-called Christian countries, those who are truly faithful to the Lord will inevitably be hated by many. As the return of the Lord draws nearer, the disciples of Jesus are sure to be hated with growing intensity.

Should our hearts ache because we are hated by the world? No! Not only should we not feel miserable or grieved but rather we should rejoice and be glad. There are two reasons for this. First, since we are hated by the world we are more assured that we do belong to Christ and are faithful to Him. Second, the promise of the Lord is that our reward will be great in heaven because of this: "Blessed are you when men hate you, and ostracize you, and heap insults upon you, and spurn your name as evil, for the sake of the Son of Man. Be glad in that day, and leap for joy, for behold, your reward is great in heaven; for in the same way their fathers used to treat the prophets."[10] That precious promise brings us great joy and hope and strength and courage, so that we should not fear the hatred of the world nor devise ways to escape from it. When we are hated, we should not regard it as shameful and regrettable, but look at it as an honor and blessing. Because our Lord never spoke a lie, He would not take back His own words. What He says, He will do; what He promises, He will accomplish. Since He promised us that if we were hated and reviled and rejected for His name's sake, our reward in heaven would be great, then we must believe one hundred percent in what He said. If we do, our hearts will immediately be filled with joy.

But we must be aware of a certain danger. Never, never should we be hated because of our own ignorance, wrongdoing or sin. We should certainly never count that kind of persecution as being for the sake of the Lord's name. Nor should we think that the great reward will be given to those who have been persecuted on those accounts. The Lord promised that the great reward is prepared for Christians who are hated specifically for His name's sake and not because of their own ignorance or sins. There is clearly a great difference between these two. We should not confuse them. The Bible has an unmistakable teaching on this: "If you are reviled for the name of Christ, you are blessed, because the Spirit of glory and of God rests upon you. By no means let any of you suffer as a murderer, or thief, or evildoer, or a troublesome meddler; but if anyone suffers as a Christian, let him not feel ashamed, but in that name let him glorify God."[11]

Unfortunately many Christians do suffer because of their own ignorance, transgressions and sins and yet consider themselves as being persecuted for the Lord's sake. For instance, many Christians are dishonest, lying, greedy for unjust money, trying to tempt the opposite sex, gaining from the loss of other people, untrustworthy, insisting on their own way, disobeying rules and regulations, discourteous, not mindful of public property or money, treating people badly, talking nonsense, inviting the dislike of others. Also, some are proud; their eyes are full of themselves; they regard themselves higher than others, view others condescendingly, brag about themselves—all these are just invitations for people to attack or persecute them. Again, some are undisciplined, lazy, not prompt, irresponsible, careless, making many errors—so no wonder they are despised and rejected by others. Some are over-zealous, fanatical in their words or deeds, appear queer and odd, thus making others uncomfortable and drawing ill-feeling against themselves. But they deceive themselves that they are being persecuted and hated for the sake of the name of the Lord. In reality it is not so—they just deserve the treatment they are getting! Among them, some actually use the name of the Lord as a guise for their sin and wrongdoing. Some don't feel that they have done anything wrong. They think that since they are Christians, every time they are hated it must be for the Lord's sake. I strongly advise such people to quickly awaken and forsake their sins and ignorance. If not, they will not only continue to be hated and rejected by others today, but when they face the Lord Himself in the future, they will be judged by Him. That would be a terrible thing!

Be aware that our Lord was hated by the world and the people of the world not for such things as ignorance and sins, since He was sinless. No one could find anything wrong with Him. He dared to challenge the Jews, "Which one of you convicts Me of sin? If I speak truth, why do you not believe Me?"[12] Those who had been with Him for three years could certainly testify on His behalf. Peter wrote: "...who committed no sin, nor was any deceit found in His mouth; and while being reviled, He did not revile in return; while suffering, He uttered no threats, but kept entrusting Himself to Him who judges righteously."[13] And John wrote: "And you know that He appeared in order to take away sins; and in Him there is no sin."[14] When so many people who hated Him gathered in the chief priest's court, they accused Him, arraigned Him, but still could not find any sin in Him. Even when they brought in a false witness, they could find no evidence. The high priest knew it was impossible to find anything wrong in His conduct and life, so he said, "I adjure You by the living God, that You tell us whether you are the Christ, the Son of God." Because he invoked Him with an oath, the Lord was obliged to respond. Jesus affirmed that what he asked was true and that, furthermore, He wanted them all to know that they would "see the Son of Man sitting at the right hand of Power, and coming on the clouds of heaven."[15] Jesus was sentenced on the basis of those few words. When they transferred Him to Pilate's court, He was examined and then Pilate announced three times to the Jews that he could not find any fault in Him.[16]

This was what the life of our Lord was like on earth. This should be a pattern for us, that we might live as His disciples. Having such a blameless life as an example, we can have a powerful witness for the Lord. His expectations for us are that we will be the salt of the earth and the light of this world and thus be worthy to be hated by the world for His name's sake, to be persecuted by the world for the Lord's name, and so be able to inherit the Lord's promises.

Do you want to know whether you truly belong to Christ? Observe the reaction of the world toward you. Do you want to know whether you are faithful to the Lord in things big and small? One way to measure it is by seeing how the world regards you. Do you want to know whether you are being hated truly for the sake of the Lord's name or merely because of your own wrongdoing or faults? I suggest that you always be honest about admitting any fault or sin that other people find in you. But at all times never forget this basic truth from Jesus' lips: "If the world hates you, you know that it has hated Me before it hated you.... If they persecute Me, they will also persecute you."[17]

- - - - - - -

Background verses used in the above text:

[1] John 15:18-25
[2] John 3:19,20
[3] John 15:18
[4] John 15:19
[5] John 15:20
[6] John 15:23
[7] John 17:14-16
[8] 1 John 3:13
[9] Matthew 24:9
[10] Luke 6:22,23
[11] 1 Peter 4:14-16
[12] John 8:46
[13] 1 Peter 2:22,23
[14] 1 John 3:5
[15] Matthew 26:59-66
[16] John 18:38, 19:4-6
[17] John 15:18,20

十　　　　　　　　順服的試金石

10
Touchstone of Obedience

> *The one who does the will of God abides forever* — 1 John 2:17b.

While our Lord was in this world He clearly gave priority to fulfilling the will of God. He stated that He had come down from heaven to earth for the express purpose of doing that will.[1] The writer of the book of Hebrews also declared that when Christ came to earth He said, "Behold, I have come to do Thy will, O God."[2]

When our Lord prayed in Gethsemane, envisioning that horrible bitter cup of suffering and death ahead of Him, seeming not willing to drink it, He called upon His Father to remove it from Him. But at that same moment He was still willing and determined to do God's will. Therefore He continued praying, "...yet not as I will, but as Thou wilt."[3] If any one of us were in that situation, we would surely also have agonized with God to remove that cup from us, even if we clearly knew that the will of God was for us to drink it. We would beg God to remove it because the bitterness was so great. But our Lord did not do that. He stopped asking the Father to remove the cup, affirming that He wanted God's will to be done. From this instance we learn that even Christ had to learn step by step to obey the will of His Father.

Our Lord not only considered that doing the will of God was His duty, He also regarded it with gladness and joy. He was not arbitrarily compelled to do God's will. He joyfully did it by an act of His own will. His willingness to do God's will is just like our willingness to take our food. Some people consider food to be the most important thing in life. But our Lord said, "My food is to do the will of Him who sent Me, and to accomplish His work."[4]

No doubt when our Lord dealt with any problem, or managed any matter, He based His decisions and actions on this important principle: Is this the will of God? When He dealt with any problem, He did not consider His own benefit or loss, glory or disgrace, blessing or calamity, failure or success, safety or risk, life or death. Because of His lack of concern for these, He could discern clearly what was God's will and what was not. After perceiving that, He was able to do God's will. He was not ashamed to be called God's beloved Son in whom God was well pleased.

I feel that in general the main difficulty people face is not whether they have the *strength* to do the will of God—although that might pose some problem—but it is primarily that they are not able to discern what *is* the will of God and what is *not*.

That is not to say that God's will is hard to understand. Through the declarations of the Scriptures and the enlightenment of the Holy Spirit who dwells in the believer, we should easily be able to understand God's will. But whenever we confuse the issue by thinking about our own profit or loss, glory or disgrace, blessing or calamity, or other such matters, immediately our eyes are dimmed by them. We can no longer differentiate what is God's will and what is not. If our heart is inclined to seek for our own profit, blessing or safety, we lose sight of the real issues and deceive ourselves. We think that anything that enables us to reach the goals we have set must be the will of God. We also deceive ourselves into thinking that anything that will help us to avoid trouble is the will of God. (Even if we don't deceive ourselves in this way, the devil will try to deceive us.) If we can utterly ignore all personal consideration and not seek our own benefit, nor seek to avoid loss, we will not be deceived by these.

Sometimes our eyes are not dimmed, our hearts are not deceived, and we do clearly know what is God's will and what isn't, but as soon as we consider our own profit or loss, a raging struggle takes place within us. Yes, we may be willing to do God's will but we also want our own profit and gain. If God's will and our desires match, naturally there doesn't seem to be any problem. But if God's will and our wishes clash, there will be a war within us. If we do not have adequate spiritual preparation and determination before this battle begins, our chances for victory are very slim. We must be fully prepared before the battle cry is sounded, arming ourselves with single-mindedness to do God's will, come what may, not considering our own profit or loss. Doing God's will has a bright future. We need to advance with courage. But even if doing God's will puts us in jeopardy or danger, we should not be timid and retreat.

To say it more simply, in dealing with all problems and affairs we should hold fast to one principle: Ask no question about profit or loss but rather discern right and wrong. If it is God's will, all will be affirmative. If it is not, all will be negative. Our Lord based His life on earth on this principle. We who are His disciples should do no less.

By living according to this principle, what can we expect to encounter? Temporal loss, disgrace, danger and calamity may be unavoidable. But the ultimate result is still our gain, our glory, our blessing and peace. Because of doing God's will, our Lord suffered loss and met such calamities, even losing His life. But because of His full obedience to God, the Father raised Him from the dead, lifted Him up to His right hand, exalted Him to the highest place and gave Him the name which is above every name.[5] No one has suffered greater loss than Jesus by doing God's will. Therefore no one has received greater reward by doing God's will than He received.

Naturally, when we do God's will we should not do it just in the expectation of future reward and glory. That kind of motivation is not worthy. We should do God's will because God loved us and saved us. Even if God would not reward us in glory, we ought to be willing to do God's will. But He did indeed promise us reward and glory in the future. And so we ought to praise Him for this with hearts of gladness. Children should not decide to obey their parents because they expect their parents to provide them with new clothes and buy nourishing food. They should obey them because the parents love them, care for and bring them up. But if parents *do* voluntarily promise these provisions and other good gifts to their children, if the children refused to rejoice and thank them, that would not be reasonable.

Because of doing God's will and not considering our own profit or loss, although we might temporarily suffer some loss or calamity, ultimately the result will be gain and glory. Those who calculatingly weigh their own profit and comfort against suffering loss by doing God's will, thinking to preserve themselves from danger, will find that not only will they lose God's eventual reward, they will still come up against distress and loss. Ultimately there will be no chance of repentance; they will cry with shame, but in vain. Then they will come to acknowledge that the words of Jesus are true and trustworthy: "For whoever wishes to save his life shall lose it; but whoever loses his life for My sake shall find it."[6] But it will be too late!

Satan is not happy to see God's children doing the will of God. He will by all means seek to obstruct them and ruin them. Two of the things he does most effectively are to use personal gain to tempt them and the possibility of loss to threaten them. If they are led to be greedy for gain and fearful of loss, they are then not able to see the will of God clearly. Even if they could see it clearly, they would be reluctant to obey. We must fix our determination early and then these two devices of Satan will utterly lose their effectiveness.

What is this determination? *To obey God's will at any cost, asking nothing about the future.* May this be true of each of us. May we discern God's will and do it, girded with His strength. Amen.

Background verses used in the above text:

[1] John 6:38
[2] Hebrews 10:5-10
[3] Matthew 26:36-39,42
[4] John 4:34
[5] Philippians 2:8,9
[6] Matthew 16:25

十一 一個陰謀的返應

11
A Plot that Boomeranged

> *Indeed, it is useless to spread the net in the eyes of any bird; but they lie in wait for their own blood; they ambush their own lives. So are the ways of everyone who gains by violence; it takes away the life of its possessors* —Proverbs 1:17-19.

Selfish people the world over do not spare any course or wicked ways to hurt others in order to gain things for their own benefit. They act with malice and an unfeeling heart, even toward their benefactors and friends. They always feel that they are very smart, but they overlook the fact that our righteous and holy God hates such wicked deeds. Sooner or later He will recompense them for their sins, and it will be much harsher than what they dealt to others.

Rechab and Baanah, brothers, were commanders serving under Saul's son, Ishbosheth, who was king of Israel.[1] Their duty was to be loyal to the king, to protect him and to direct his troops in battle.

After Abner, who had been the commander-in-chief, was killed by Joab at Hebron, Ishbosheth was discouraged as he sensed his power was declining. He now needed his commanders' loyalty more than ever. They should have been faithful to him, standing by him and comforting him, urging him not to lose heart. Even if Ishbosheth were to prove unsuccessful in regaining his power, losing out in the bitter end, even then these two commanders need not have lost their respectful standing in the eyes of their fellow Israelites. Heroes are not necessarily judged by their failure or success, but rather by their faithfulness and loyalty under adverse circumstances. Who might have suspected that the hearts of these two brother commanders were so low and wicked and self-seeking as they proved to be?

Upon hearing that Abner had died in Hebron, and guessing that Ishbosheth would soon lose his position of power, they devised a strategy on how to cross over to the winning side. Without regard for loyalty or human feeling, they plotted to kill their master whom they had been serving—he who trusted them. Their wicked deed was carried out while Ishbosheth was resting in his own bedroom. They murdered him and then cut off his head, planning to bring it to David with the expectation of receiving a reward from him. This act of striking a blow against a man who was already down is most despicable. Much more so as Ishbosheth was their leader and had trusted them. We can imagine what the two were thinking on their way to David with the head of Ishbosheth. They must have anticipated that as soon as they arrived at David's palace they would receive immediate applause and reward. They might even be given a high position. Their future would be rosy from now on. They must have been full of self-esteem, thinking they had outsmarted everyone and were going to make a great profit at the expense of others.

Unexpectedly, David did not even commend them for their deed; on the contrary, he was very angry and upset with them. "Order the youths to kill them, chop off their hands and feet and hang them up by the pool in Hebron," he commanded. Because they had divided Ishbosheth's body into two pieces, David had their bodies divided into five pieces. With their own hands they had killed their master, and had carried his head to David with those same hands; they had traveled a long distance on their feet to obtain a reward—so David cut off their hands "that shed innocent blood" and their feet "that run rapidly to evil."[2] Their bodies hanging beside the pool of Hebron displayed to all that this is what happens to wicked men who plot to reap profit at the expense of others. God had this incident recorded through His servant to let people of all generations know the pitiful end of wicked men, so that others might be forewarned lest they follow in their footsteps.

Notice David's heart and character. He had been persecuted and pursued by Saul for many years, tasting much hardship and distress as a result. Yet he did not even take vengeance on Saul, twice sparing Saul's life when he could have killed him. When the news of the death of Saul and three of his sons on the battlefield reached his ears, in his grief he wrote a eulogy to honor them. His dealings with Saul could be described as "virtue and righteousness personified." After the death of Saul, the Israelites had crowned his son Ishbosheth as king, but the people of Judah had crowned David as king. So it happened that "there was a long war between the house of Saul and the house of David."[3] If someone of less character had been in the position of David when Baanah and Rechab came to him after their act, he would probably have been very glad and rewarded them greatly for getting rid of the one who stood between him and a united kingdom. But David was not the kind of person to consider his own benefit. What he valued most was the will of God and righteousness and truth. No wonder the Lord praised David many times, calling him "a man after God's own heart" and showing mercy to his descendants because of him.

How many on earth are like Baanah and Rechab—selfish, vulgar and wicked! When a person is in a position of power and wealth, many flatter him, bow to him, serve and run errands for him to show their loyalty and respect. But when the day comes that he loses his position of power and wealth, and needs the help and sympathy of others, his former "friends" will not come to assist him or comfort him. On the contrary, they may add insult to injury and exploit him for spoil, attack him, insult him, stoop to take away whatever bit of property he might be depending on for his livelihood—yes, and even take from him his very life. These exploiters excuse themselves, saying, "He is getting just what he deserves." Maybe what they say is true, but we ask them, "If that man was so bad, why, in his time of prosperity, did you flatter him, honor him, serve him, show loyalty and respect for him?" Naturally they will make up some story to gloss over their vulgar and wicked actions. But God is not mocked. As God judged these two wicked brothers, so He will also judge vulgar and crooked men anywhere and anytime.

When Baanah and Rechab assassinated their master, they surely felt their scheme to obtain reward was foolproof, never supposing that it would cost them their lives. Even if they failed to attain their full reward, they never dreamed that they would fall into such a disaster as did befall them. Throughout history many people have relied on their own wisdom and plotted against others, hoping to gain something for themselves. Because they expect success from their evil efforts, they go around happy and confident. They never imagine that something terrible might happen to them—that the plot might boomerang and hurt them even more than those they intend to injure. Had Baanah or Rechab suspected what gruesome thing was to befall them, they would have regretted and abandoned their faulty plan—but perhaps too late.

To be like these wicked commanders may not, in today's world, be as mortally dangerous as it was in the days of David. Today it is not common, even rare, for people like David who are upright and just to take physical revenge on their enemies in such terrible ways. Forceful men like Rechab and Baanah might find themselves being treated royally wherever they go—held in high respect because they know how to eliminate their enemies and advance themselves into positions of power. But such popularity does not last; violence will catch up with the violent in due time. Justice will eventually have its way.

Those who might have use for such men, though they accept their services and applaud them for valor, will not trust traitors very long. They will always be suspicious and think to themselves, *When you saw your former master in trouble and facing defeat, you dared to kill him and desert to my side; the same thing could happen if one day I should become weak in my position and face defeat. If you did it before, you will probably do it again.* In today's world, though it is hard to find upright men like David, you will find plenty of people everywhere who are looking out for themselves. Should people like these two wicked brothers encounter an upright person like David, they cannot escape the judgment they deserve. For no matter how the world changes, God's righteousness will not change; wherever there are upright people, God will use them to work justice for Himself. But if there are no such people available, God will resort to wicked ones to accomplish His justice for Him. No matter what the circumstances, people like Rechab and Baanah will never get away with their evil deeds.

People love themselves; therefore they injure others. The fact is, that in injuring others they ultimately injure themselves. Does that mean that we should not love ourselves? Not at all! We *should* love ourselves. In doing so we are going in the right direction, but only if in loving ourselves we do not injure others. Much good ought to be done. If we love not only ourselves but also those around us, there is no risk involved and much good may come from it.

If we love others, naturally we will receive love from them. If we are faithful to others, naturally they will trust us. But not only will those who personally receive benefit from us love and trust us, but also those people who see our faithfulness toward their friends will respect us and trust us. One day when they have some special need, they will remember us and our faithfulness. They will know that because we were faithful to our old friends we will also be faithful to new friends, associates, business partners or co-workers. A faithful person who "loves his neighbor as himself," no matter in what generation or environment he lives, is a most safe, blessed, respected and trusted man.

Many people consider an opportunist to be a wise man. The fact is, he is a most foolish man. Many consider that one who injures others to gain personal profit is smart. The fact is, he will end up most pitifully. It is only the faithful and loyal person who is a truly wise man. Only the person who genuinely loves others can receive the greatest benefit. Look at the record of Baanah and Rechab and take serious heed to the result of their opportunism. Should not this reminder make us fear and tremble lest we slip into their way of thinking?

Background verses used in the above text:
[1] 2 Samuel 4:1-12
[2] Proverbs 6:17,18
[3] 2 Samuel 3:1

十二  决志

12
Determination

Therefore, my beloved brethren, be steadfast, immovable, always abounding in the work of the Lord —1 Corinthians 15:58a.

In the days of Daniel, recorded in the Old Testament, three Hebrew men who were appointed administrators over Babylon under the rule of King Nebuchadnezzar dared to stand against him. Shadrach, Meshach and Abed-nego violated the command of the king to worship the golden image that he had set up. As a result, they were thrown into the fiery furnace, but through God's miraculous intervention they were safely delivered. God's name was glorified and the three men were greatly blessed.

Throughout history, believers have been inspired and encouraged by this story and often I have used it to bring out many important truths to build up Christians. There is still another vital truth that we can learn from this episode that relates to the relationship between our determination to obey God and the victory that we wish to gain. The Hebrew men replied to the king that they really didn't need to give him an answer because they would not, under any circumstances, worship his golden image. And whether or not their God saw fit to deliver them from the blazing fire was of no consequence—they would still not change their minds.[1] With what strength they stated it! How courageously! "We are not going to serve your gods or worship the golden image...." There was no debate about it, no hesitation. As far as they were concerned, the decision had already been made through the preparation of their character and their firm faith. Imagine, before a king as powerful as Nebuchadnezzar, who reigned over the whole nation and had the power of life and death in his hands, they dared to speak so brashly. Some might think that in their position the three men went a little too far, were really a bit foolish. Couldn't they have spoken more gently and tactfully in answering the king? Then he might not have come down so hard on them. A wiser approach might not have incited the king's anger so hotly and they might have escaped the harm that was in store for them. Those who reason thus have not paid close attention to the circumstances. The decree of the king had already been issued. There were only two paths presented to the three men: One was to fall down and worship the image and be safe; the other was to refuse and immediately be cast into the blazing furnace. No matter how tactfully they formed their answer, the consequences would have been the same.

Likewise today, the problem we face in our own Christian position regarding our stand of obedience to God is not whether we decide to use gentle, reasonable and tactful words to refuse but whether we will "worship the image" or not. Naturally, if the attitude of the three men had been more gentle and tactful, maybe the king would not have been "filled with wrath."[2] But what really would have been the difference? The three would have been cast into the furnace just the same. The firm determination of the men did not increase their ill-fated persecution but rather paved the way for them to be victorious through it. Why was this so?

Notice that the king gave the men another chance when they came before him, his words being clearly phrased to help acquit them, hoping they would submit and reconsider. "Now if you are ready...at the moment you hear the music...fall down and worship the image...."[3] They had already offended his decrees and he certainly was not obligated to give them a second chance. But the king doubtless disliked to see them burned to death, for after all, they were his officials and men of special expertise.[4] The king had favored them and promoted them to important positions; certainly it should be no surprise that he would try to provide a way out for them and protect them from harm. It was clearly too late for his decree to be rescinded. His reputation was at stake. So he used this strategy on the one hand to maintain his prestige and on the other to preserve the three men. He probably thought he could attain two advantages with one move. As wise as the three men were reputed to be, they certainly understood what the king had in mind. If their determination had been even a little unsteady, possibly they would have backed down under the king's threat of severe punishment. They might have been grateful for the king's generosity and softened their stand. But if their will had been shaky, it would have led to compromise and then from compromise to submission. The result would have been that they would end up serving the god that Nebuchadnezzar served and worshiping the golden image that he had erected.

Can you see the situation clearly now? The firm determination of the three men was absolutely necessary. And it was because of that resolve that they went on to achieve glorious victory. True, their unyielding attitude aroused the king's wrath, but it was not his wrath that hurt them. His wrath actually contributed to manifesting the glory of God all the more. Because the king was so angry, the furnace was heated seven times hotter than usual.[5] That caused the great power and work of God to show forth all the more because the furnace was so hot that the soldiers who carried the men were burned to death. That proved that the three men who were cast into the furnace should certainly have been burned to ashes. But something unexpected happened! A fourth man walked with them in the fire, "...like a son of the gods!"[6] If the furnace had not been that obviously hot, some might have rationalized that it was really not hot enough to have burned them up. So they might have said this was not really the work of God. Now, without question it was a miracle. This incident confirms God's words, "For the wrath of man shall praise Thee...."[7]

When any one of God's people confronts temptation, he should express the same firm determination. If he knows clearly that a certain thing is not pleasing to God, he should firmly resist it without hesitation, without second thoughts, not fearing the consequences nor the wrath of others. Especially should there be no fear of personal risk or loss. If we hesitate even a little at such a serious juncture, Satan will use all sorts of wiles, through others, tempting us and leading us to go astray. He will try to weaken our resolve through our own tender flesh and our desire for self-preservation. The result will be disastrous!

We know that some believers who know without question that something is not in accord with God's truth nevertheless beg for time to consider the issue. They actually say that they will pray about it and see what God shows them and how He might guide them. Isn't this clearly tempting God? They already know that it is a black-and-white, clear-cut issue, but they still stall for time. Would God lead them to do something that is not in agreement with the truth? The reason they stall is twofold: First, for their own benefit; second, to somehow avoid personal harm. Otherwise they would not ask for some special indication from God contrary to what they know He already has set before them. Are they hoping that God will change His mind or His will just to accommodate them, to benefit them or help them escape from harm? What can be gained by this delay to make a decision? Certainly God can't change His will. But neither will God force them to submit. So He just lets them alone and consequently they begin to fall into sin.

In ancient times the prophet Balaam had a similar experience. When Balak was king of Moab, he sent for Balaam to come and curse the Israelites. Balaam asked the Lord about it and the Lord clearly told him not to. He obeyed God's word the first time and declined the invitation of Balak's men to go along with them. Another invitation was issued to him and this time he hesitated, saying, "I will find out what else the Lord will speak to me."[8] He had already found God's clear will in the matter. He was not allowed to curse a people whom God wanted blessed. But because of the persistence of the invitations and the promise of benefit to himself in reward by the king,

Determination 93

he wanted a second opinion from God. Would the Lord change His mind just for Balaam's benefit? His greedy heart was touched and he harbored the hope that God would alter His will. So he began to walk that risky road. Finally, because of Balak's deviousness, Balaam betrayed the Israelites and brought down the wrath of God. Balaam, far from benefiting personally, was killed under the sword of the Israelites.[9]

A believer who already knows the will of God and yet does not firmly obey it, shows that his heart is already distracted and greedy or fearful. In such a case, failure is inevitable. When the three Hebrews expressed their unchanging determination before the king, their hearts were very true to God with not a hint of greediness, fear, or consideration for their own gain or loss, benefit or risk. All they knew was to respect God and be loyal to Him. When we see such stability we can be sure that the believer will be victorious in his battle.

Once I received a letter from a young Christian lady from another city. She wrote: "...A few days ago temptation came to me. Thank God for His grace that reminded me about the principle of the Bible about which you often made us aware: No matter how eloquent or enticing are the words of people, because of respect for God our obedience to God must be complete. Several times I have declined to be introduced to a non-believer for the purpose of considering marriage. I told my colleagues and friends and relatives that I am a Christian and I will absolutely not be yoked with an unbeliever, all the more so in marriage. So now they don't attempt that any more. There were also some others facing the same issue, who did not hear of my stand firsthand but were informed by those who knew of it, and now they don't pursue that course any more. Thank God that He helped me to be victorious through it all...."

How refreshing! How constant her stand from the beginning! Her attitude was just the same as that of the three Hebrew men. Therefore she also had the same victory as they. To have victory over temptation one must have this established determination, otherwise one fails in every step; things go from bad to worse and finally end up in utter defeat.

Many Christians confronting such temptations would be inclined to say, "Wait a minute, let me consider. Let me ask God and see how He leads me." In a case such as this girl faced, some Christians indeed would want to first meet the other party face to face and maybe talk it over. If the other party was not to their liking, they'd say that it was not God's will and proceed to reject the possibility. However, if it turned out that the other party was to their liking, they would ask God once again to see how He would lead them. This is not genuinely asking God, much less sincerely asking for God's guidance. This is having one's mind and plan already made up and petitioning God to grant His agreement with our decision. This is taking the road of one's own tastes and asking God to confirm it. In such a circumstance, God has no way to show them His way, no way to guide them. God can only abandon them to follow their own devices.

There are also some Christians who perhaps go one step further. They would not think of tempting God in that way; they would be willing to obey God, but they would not be willing to embarrass or offend others involved. They would be reluctant to say outright, "Absolutely not!" They seek for some tactful excuse, thinking to make their refusal more palatable to others. They might promise to consider the matter, or they might say that they have to talk it over with others, or pray about it for a while, although in their mind they have already decided to reject it. Now they are committing the sin of lying on top of their evasiveness. The devil will attack them from *this* vantage point now, by using the weakness of their flesh and causing them to give second thoughts after all, and by involving others in a decision that they should be making alone. Their original decision begins to get shaky. When they first promised to "consider" the matter they were not really serious about doing that, but only used the chance to respond with more tact to the circumstances. Now it turns out that they *are* actually "considering" it. In the first battle they were already defeated and so in the ensuing one they may also be easily defeated. Their failure becomes almost inevitable.

By first observing how a Christian starts out to deal with a temptation, we can just about tell, with seventy or eighty percent accuracy, whether he is going to fail or be victorious. Of those who are not firm in the very beginning in dealing with temptation, very few come out victorious from the battle. Knowing that there is an intimate relationship between firm determination and the victorious life, we should,

Determination

by the grace of God, learn from the three Hebrew men and follow their example of steadfastness, irrevocable choice, courage, faithfulness to God and lack of concern for themselves. Whenever we are tempted to sin against God we must say, without hesitation, "Absolutely not! Absolutely not!"

- - - - - - -

Background verses used in the above text:
[1] Daniel 3:16-18
[2] Daniel 3:19
[3] Daniel 3:15
[4] Daniel 1:17-20
[5] Daniel 3:19
[6] Daniel 3:24-27
[7] Psalm 76:10
[8] Numbers 22:19
[9] Numbers 31:7,8, 14-16

十三

奇人與奇事

13

Strange Men & Amazing Miracles

> God has chosen the foolish things of the world to shame the wise, and God has chosen the weak things of the world to shame the things which are strong, and the base things of the world and the despised, God has chosen, the things that are not, that He might nullify the things that are, that no man should boast before God —1 Corinthians 1:27-29.

That small band of apostles was made up of truly wonderful men. Because they boldly preached Jesus, they were arrested by the high priest and his associates and put into jail. During the night they were led out of prison by an angel. Ordinary men would probably have wanted to run far away after that and hide in some secret place so as not to be discovered and arrested again. But when morning came, these men obeyed the words of the angel, "Go your way, stand and speak to the people in the temple the whole message of this Life."[1]

Didn't these men realize that if they were arrested again, besides facing their original charges they would have one more added, that of escaping from jail? Moreover, after being released they had still persisted in preaching Jesus. That would certainly incite even greater anger in the enemy and they would face still greater persecution. Weren't they aware of this? Here they were, risking harm and danger without hesitation. They kept right on advancing. What a strange band of men!

Yes, they might be thought of as strange in the eyes of men, but not in God's sight. This was exactly what He demanded of those who belonged to Him. He wanted them to care for nothing but doing His will and accomplishing His work. He wanted them to have no anxiety, no fear or personal ambition, only to concentrate on pleasing Him and being faithful to Him. Those apostles did just that. Although they were fresh out of prison, as soon as they heard the angel command them to preach in the temple, "about daybreak" they started to do so. Their actions expressed how faithful, obedient and courageous they were! They didn't consider their own lives nor their own exhaustion. They didn't even return to their homes first to have a good night's sleep, to overcome their physical fatigue. Neither did they discuss the matter among themselves to see whether they should take the risk of preaching the resurrection of Christ again. As soon as they received the command of God through the angel, they obeyed! Wasn't God pleased with such people? We shouldn't wonder that they were greatly used of God. God would certainly manifest His glory and strength through them. They were "strange" people and so God worked strange signs and wonders through them.

While they were preaching in the temple, the high priest and his officials were gathered in the Council chamber adjacent to the temple. They sent men to bring the apostles out to them, but an unexpected thing was reported: the prison gates were still locked quite securely and the guards were standing properly at their posts, but when they opened the prison they found no one inside. The men returned with this report to the surprised priests. They didn't know what to do. At that moment someone came in with the news that the men whom they had been holding in prison were standing in the temple and teaching the people. The captain of the temple guard and his men went to the temple and brought them back to stand before the Council. The high priest addressed them, "We gave you strict orders not to continue teaching in this name, and behold, you have filled Jerusalem with your teaching and intend to bring this man's blood upon us."

The high priest flaunted his authority. Were the apostles frightened by it? Not a bit. Their own reply was more severe and powerful than the words of the high priest. They said, "We must obey God rather than men." How courageous! This truly should be the principle for every child of God in dealing with anything and everything. Of course this doesn't mean that Christians should not submit to higher powers. "Let every person be in subjection to the governing authorities."[2] "Submit yourselves for the Lord's sake to every human institution."[3] The former are the words of Paul and the latter are the words of Peter, the very same Peter who was advocating not obeying the authority of the high priest on this occasion. Was Peter contradicting himself? Not at all. Only when men's authority doesn't contradict God's command should we be fully obedient to men's authority. Otherwise we can only obey God rather than men. God clearly commanded the apostles to spread the gospel of Christ and the high priest forbade them to preach this truth. If Peter and the other apostles were to obey God, then they could not obey the high priest. If they obeyed the high priest, then they couldn't obey God. Under such circumstances, they had no alternative.

The high priest and his men were afraid that the blood of Jesus was going to be laid to their charge...and now the apostles were directly accusing them of having Jesus put to death by hanging Him on the cross. They openly stated that Jesus whom they killed was now exalted by God as Saviour. Those words struck so hard at the high priest and his men that they could no longer bear it. No wonder that when the Council heard this they were furious and wanted to get rid of them.

When I read this portion of Scripture, my heart is overwhelmed with boundless respect and admiration. These were fearless men, in spite of imprisonment, accusations and threats; they were speaking what God wanted them to speak. Because of such people the gospel spread everywhere and the church was established. Today we too [in China] have a chance to hear the gospel and to believe in Christ because of them.

The fury of the authorities was reaching its peak. This time the apostles were threatened with death. But if God does not permit it, not a hair from our heads will fall to the ground.[4] At that critical moment a person appeared on the scene to speak out. A Pharisee named Gamaliel, a teacher of the Law, respected by all the people, stood up in the Council and gave orders to put the men outside for a short time. And he said to them, "Men of Israel, take care what you propose to do with these men." Then he cited two examples of rebellious leaders as precedents. These had risen up from the ranks and gained a following, but since they were not of God, they and their followers had soon been scattered and their plans proved unsuccessful. He therefore offered the following strategy: "And so in the present case, I say to you, stay away from these men and let them alone, for if this plan or action should be of men, it will be overthrown; but if it is of God, you will not be able to overthrow them; or else you may be found fighting against God."[5]

This man's words stated an enduring truth that is applicable to any generation: If anything is of God, no one can destroy it. The Jews attacked the apostles with every means at their disposal and persecuted the church. But they couldn't destroy the church and the gospel kept spreading further and gaining momentum not only throughout Jerusalem but through all Judea and then to Rome. The Roman Emperor and all the powers of Rome attacked God's messengers and the gospel, persecuting the church. From the year 64 A.D. to 313 A.D.—over two hundred years—many believers were tortured, imprisoned, exiled, killed because of their faith in Christ. Humanly speaking, Christians should long ago have disappeared from the earth. On the contrary, followers of Christ have increased more and more. The gospel was constantly preached far and wide, until early in the fourth century even the Roman Emperor, Constantine, bowed down before Christ. From the historical facts, however, we understand that though Constantine made an appearance of submitting to Christ, he apparently was not a true believer in Christ but sought rather to make use of Christianity for his own ends. Whether he truly believed or merely took advantage of the gospel, the church of Christ could not be destroyed by men. This has been obvious throughout the ages.

From the early fourth century until now is a span of over sixteen hundred years. Through all of this long period the gospel has been preached without interruption. The church of Christ has also been continuously under attack by its opponents and made use of by ambitious people. But the gospel is being preached now to people in every corner of the world, fulfilling the words of Jesus: "And this gospel of the kingdom shall be preached in the whole world for a witness to all the nations, and then the end shall come."[6] This solid fact proves the truth of what Gamaliel stated. It has been attested from history that no one has the authority to oppose God and no one can destroy the work of God.

Were the words of Gamaliel taken seriously in the Council? Yes, they were very effective. The Council took his advice and God saved the apostles from critical danger through his speech. What connection did Gamaliel have with the apostles? The apostle Paul had been a student of Gamaliel.[7] As the young Saul, he persecuted the church with all his might and killed many Christians. How was it that Saul, who was imprisoning those who believed in Christ and flogging them in the courts, was not deterred from such actions by his teacher? The attitude of Gamaliel toward the Christians is, in light of this, not hard to guess. Even though Gamaliel was not forthrightly against the Christians, he probably would never have actually sided with them or protected them. Doubtless he was no sympathizer with the Christians. But on that particular day God needed the speech of such an influential person to save the apostles from the hands of the Jews, and He used Gamaliel. Isn't that a strange and marvelous thing?

God uses all kinds of people and events to accomplish His will or to save those who fear Him or punish those who rebel against Him. All of the human race is under His control. He can use anyone to accomplish His work. Since then, although many resist and oppose God, yet God turns it around to accomplish His will. When we fully understand this truth, we should not be afraid or anxious about anything, only concentrate on pleasing God and doing His will and work. *We* will see God work out His salvation *in us* to manifest His glory even as in former days He worked in the lives of the apostles.

And we know that through those strange apostles God performed strange signs.

There is another thing we should notice. God can even rescue us through unbelievers, although He does not want us to look to them nor seek their help. The apostles didn't ask Gamaliel to help them. They probably didn't even suspect that he would deliver such a speech. If we anticipate or solicit the help of unbelievers and plead for their assistance, God will not help us through them. Also He might change His face toward us and let those in whom we trusted and hoped become our shame and calamity. The Bible has clear teaching on this principle: "Woe to the rebellious children," declares the Lord, "who execute a plan, but not Mine, and make an alliance, but not of My Spirit, in order to add sin to sin; who proceed down to Egypt, without consulting Me, to take refuge in the safety of Pharaoh, and to seek shelter in the shadow of Egypt! Therefore the safety of Pharaoh will be your shame, and the shelter in the shadow of Egypt, your humiliation."[8] When the Israelites were attacked by the enemy, they should have looked to God and waited upon God. If they had done so, God would surely have delivered them. Unfortunately they didn't, but they went down to Egypt for help instead. Because they depended on men and not God, God was angry with them and allowed them to be put to shame. Those people were "not for help or profit, but for shame and also for reproach."[9] "Now the Egyptians are men and not God, and their horses are flesh and not spirit. So the Lord will stretch out His hand, and he who helps will stumble and he who is helped will fall, and all of them will come to an end together."[10]

Yes, God can use all sorts of people to help us. But we should rely solely on God and never ask for help from godless men. If we do, that proves that we don't trust and honor God. Also, because of that we would appear to be trying to please men, thus disobeying God's command. We could then be easily exploited and used. We must be very careful about this.

God did not allow the apostles to be killed but He did permit them to be flogged. He did not prevent that in His perfect will. Because the church at that time was in dire need of the guidance and nurture of the apostles, if all of them had been killed by the Jews on that occasion, the church which was only laying its foundations would not only have lost powerful leaders but also the accurate teaching needed to establish a firm base. Therefore God had to protect this brave group of apostles so that they would not be eliminated by the Jews. As to the flogging, it was not a loss to the apostles but rather for their profit. Notice their attitude after they were flogged: "They went on their way from the presence of the Council, rejoicing that they had been considered worthy to suffer shame for His name."[11] Humanly speaking, a group of adults who had been beaten by such an authoritative Council, under the gaze of all, might naturally have reacted with shame and remorse. Those apostles didn't even feel sorry for themselves but rather rejoiced to "suffer shame for His name."

What was "this name" for which they were willing to suffer such humiliation? It is the name of Jesus Christ of whom Paul wrote: "Therefore also God highly exalted Him, and bestowed on Him the name which is above every name, that at the name of Jesus every knee should bow, of those who are in heaven, and on earth, and under the earth, and that every tongue should confess that Jesus Christ is Lord, to the glory of the Father."[12] Is there anyone in the world worthy to suffer shame for this wonderfully honored and great name? No one. But God allowed the apostles to suffer shame for this name, not because they were worthy but "had been considered worthy...." How could they not keep from rejoicing at such a privilege?

When some Christians suffer a little shame or antagonism or jeers or ridicule for the Lord's name, they feel that it is so distasteful and hard to bear. And other Christians do everything they can to escape such things—so they become afraid even to confess the Lord's name before men. This is certainly because they have not fully comprehended that the Lord's name is such a noble and great name. They do not understand that to suffer for "this name" is a truly glorious thing! If they fully grasped the fact that this name is above every name, and that when that day comes, the very angels from heaven and all the living beings on earth and the dead under the earth will all fall down on their knees and acknowledge that Jesus Christ is Lord, they would be just like the apostles, "rejoicing that they had been considered worthy to suffer shame for His name."

After the apostles were beaten, what did the Council say to them?

They "ordered them to speak no more in the name of Jesus." Did they obey this time? No! They couldn't obey nor should they have obeyed. "But to the degree that you share the sufferings of Christ, keep on rejoicing; so that also at the revelation of His glory, you may rejoice with exultation."[13] Every day, in the temple and from house to house, they kept right on teaching and preaching Jesus as the Christ. Because the apostles expressed such perfect obedience, faithfulness and boldness, no wonder God did great things through them.

Yes, preaching the gospel is the command of the Lord and it is our duty to proclaim it to the saving of souls. Nothing should prevent us from preaching the gospel, nor does anyone have the authority to interfere with our witness to the resurrected Lord. If someone forbids us to teach people in his name, we must answer, "We must obey God rather than men." We should not be afraid of anybody, because God is with us. He is responsible to protect those who are faithful to Him. God worked great miracles in the days of the early church to save and protect those faithful ones. Today He is still working the same miracles. He is the faithful God, the unchanging God. If we are put to shame and attacked for the Lord's sake, we too should rejoice and be glad because the promises in the Bible will be fulfilled in us: "Blessed are you when men revile you, and persecute you, and say all kinds of evil against you falsely, on account of Me. Rejoice, and be glad, for your reward in heaven is great, for so they persecuted the prophets who were before you."[14]

- - - - - - -

Background verses used in the above text:

[1] Acts 5:12-42
[2] Romans 13:1-7
[3] 1 Peter 2:13-17
[4] Acts 27:34
[5] Acts 5:38,39
[6] Matthew 24:14
[7] Acts 22:3
[8] Isaiah 30:1-3
[9] Isaiah 30:5
[10] Isaiah 31:1-3
[11] Acts 5:41
[12] Philippians 2:9-11
[13] 1 Peter 4:13
[14] Matthew 5:11,12

14

The Echoes of Life

"Whatever you want others to do for you, do so for them, for this is the Law and the Prophets" —Matthew 7:12.

After his father Jacob passed away, Joseph took his body back to the land of Canaan in accord with the promise made to his father on his deathbed.[1] At first glance, this may seem to be a simple statement about a happening that presented no special difficulty. But if we look at the episode more carefully, we will realize that it was not at all an easy promise to fulfill. Transportation in those days was far different from the present situation. Today we have trains, cars, planes...and a trip of several hundred miles is no great hardship. It was not so easy in those ancient days. To travel on land, the only means of transportation besides walking was by carriage, on horseback, or by camel. From Egypt to Canaan, about two hundred miles, would take people quite a while. Much of the way was desert, and many hardships could be expected; besides, there was the inconvenience of obtaining food and lodging along the way for such a great number of people as accompanied Joseph.

Joseph had enjoyed the respect of all in Egypt for over twenty years, while bearing the heavy responsibilities of Egypt's administration—probably living a comfortable and good life, as befitted his position in the government. When his father passed away, Joseph was about fifty-six years old. To take his father's body to Canaan was quite a complicated task. But because of his father's wishes, and the promise he had made to him, he did not try to avoid those difficulties but went ahead and made all the arrangements. He and his brothers accomplished the rigorous journey and buried the body in the cave of Machpelah where his other ancestors were buried. This son fulfilled his promise to his late father.

Another fifty-some years passed, and when it came time for Joseph to die he also charged his kinsmen that when they, under God's care, would depart from Egypt, they should carry his bones back to Canaan with them—similar to what his father had charged him.[2] How did his descendants respond? When it became possible for them to fulfill their promise they did so, though they had to wait several generations until the Egyptians allowed the children of Israel to leave the land.

Moses was born long after Joseph's death, so he had neither heard Joseph's voice nor seen him; he had only heard his forebears relate his dying request. Nevertheless, he felt bound to keep that promise, even under such a difficult and dramatic situation as the exodus. For in their haste to leave it was hard enough to consider caring for the living, without being concerned about the bones of one who had died two hundred years before.[3] But as Joseph was faithful to *his* dying father, so his descendants were also faithful to *him*. As he had treated *his* aged father, so *he* got treated in turn. As the Bible says, in a different context, "Do not be deceived, God is not mocked; for whatever a man sows, this he will also reap."[4] And, "Whatever measure you deal out to others, it will be dealt to you in return."[5]

When Joseph was burying his father in Canaan he may not have been thinking of his own later situation, since he was only in his fifties, but his act of faithfulness resulted in his reaping personal benefit too. Not only does *God* treat us reciprocally, but how people treat us and how we treat them are interrelated. The facts speak: A kind person will be treated with kindness; a rude person will be treated rudely; a faithful person will be treated faithfully; a crafty person will be treated with craftiness. Joseph was a faithful person and he was treated faithfully by others.

When you stand in a valley and shout, "Brother, I think well of you—I love you!" you will hear from afar the echo of the same. If you shout again, "You disreputable person, you disgust me. Death to you!" you will hear the echo return your words. Who is responding to you? No one—only your echo. Whatever you say, the same will return to you. By the same token, whatever you are receiving daily in life is but a reflection of what you give. If you have been treating people kindly, they will be treating you kindly in return. If you treat people faithfully, they will treat you the same. Although treating people with faith and kindness does not *guarantee* that you will receive the respect and confidence of others, yet one who is respected and trusted by others surely must be treating others with kindness and faith already.

When Joseph showed respect for his father, his children also expressed the same to him. This pattern can be seen in many homes. If you yourself respect your parents, although you haven't directly taught your children this practice in so many words, your daily life and deeds will give your children a practical example. If you respect and obey your parents, your children will see your life day by day and naturally come to understand how they should respect their parents. If, on the other hand, you are rebellious and disparage your parents and yet try to teach your children to honor and obey you, they not only will refuse to respect you but are likely to say behind your back, "Is this reasonable? He doesn't respect *his* parents; why should he expect us to respect *him?* That's impossible!" The sage has well said: "If you are right yourself, you will be obeyed without having to command others to do so; if you yourself are not right, even should you command it, you won't be obeyed."

The story is told that at a certain place there was a man who did not respect his parents. His mother passed away and left the aged father, who was still healthy. The son loved his wife and children but unfortunately treated his father with disgust. He listened to what his wife told him and did not even permit his aged father to eat at the same table with them. Once his father had accidently broken a bowl. That aggravated the couple's anger. From that day on, they wouldn't let his father eat from a bowl. The son prepared a tin can for his father and filled it with food for him at every meal. But he and his wife and children used beautiful chinaware. The aged father was very hurt, but because he lived with his son, even though he was grieved and angry he dared not speak out.

One day the man returned home and saw his eight-year-old son with a pair of scissors and a big tin can. He was trying to cut the tin can. The father was afraid that his son would hurt himself and asked him to put the scissors down. But his son persisted. He asked his son what he had in mind for the tin can. His young son answered, "Daddy, I know you eat more than grandpa. Today I found this tin can which is much larger than the one grandpa uses for his meals. Therefore I want to cut it smooth so that I can keep it, and when you grow old I can use it to give you your meals." This man was shocked and dismayed at what his son said and suddenly came to himself. He was afraid that when he became old he would receive this unwelcome treatment from his own son. He promptly repented of his wrong attitude and deeds and immediately confessed it to his aged father. From then on he earnestly respected his father, going out of his way to make him happy.

That man was surely blessed to have such a discerning and loving son rescue him before it was too late. The majority of people who are disrespectful to their parents haven't such good fortune. Only when they themselves grow old do they weep bitterly, recalling their disrespect for their parents, which then cannot be undone.

Many people scold their children because they are stubborn and willful and blame them for their ungratefulness and lack of conscience. Actually, what they are reaping is merely the harvest of the seeds which they sowed many years before. If they had not been stubborn, willful, ungrateful and lacking in conscience some twenty or thirty years before, their children would not be treating them like they are today.

As in the family, so in society. Would a person who has no concern for trustworthiness, who does not speak the truth, who advocates cunning devices, plays tricks and so forth, expect others to trust him, depend on him, form loyal friendships with him, and deal with him sincerely? Can a person who has been selfish all along, with no concern for others, even harming others in order to gain his own benefit, expect others to look after him, love and protect him, help him in time of need and rescue him in time of danger? Can a person who is greedy for money, practicing embezzlement, smuggling, seizing others by force, expect others to cooperate with him and entrust their money and business to him? Can a person who is actually frivolous, a dirty talker, fond of women, expect others to respect him and invite him into their homes? Can a person who often talks nonsense and is irresponsible, passing on rumors, losing people's confidence by lying, expect that what he says will be taken seriously and carry weight? Can a person who is usually inconsistent, changeable—today treating a person as a bosom friend, tomorrow as his enemy—expect to have trusted friends to share his joy and sorrow? If you plant thistles, you will never reap grapes; if you plant thorns, you will never reap figs. If you plant bad seeds of deceit and lies, hurt others for selfish gain, are greedy and thieving, promiscuous and lewd, faithless, promise-breaking and treacherous, you will absolutely not reap other people's trust, commitment, respect and kindness. The words of the Scriptures never fail.

Let us notice another thing: From the time Joseph kept the promise to his dying father until the day Moses brought Joseph's bones out of Egypt, there was a span of about two hundred years. But Moses remembered the dying command of his forefather. Truly that is something out of the ordinary. That Joseph's filial piety in keeping his promise was handed down among the Jews for so long is a very significant fact. The Israelites undoubtedly forgot, over such a long period of time, most of the words spoken by their forebears, but what their forebears *did* moved them to songs and tears and was thus easily perpetuated from one generation to the other. Because of this, the dying command of Joseph was also deeply ingrained in the hearts of the Israelites and remembered.

History shows that a person's good words must be in line with his conduct in order to have a deep and lasting effect on people, not only now but for years to come. Certainly it is desirable that preachers be able to preach fine expository sermons; but their high character and holy lifestyle is more important. It is this practical expression that helps people keep in mind the truth they are receiving through their words. Though a preacher's exact words may be forgotten, his exemplary conduct and character will remind people of what he said. Have you seen people who were obviously trusted by others, who even were entrusted with the possessions of others—people respected and loved? That never comes about by happenstance. They have probably paid a great price to acquire this trust. For years they certainly have been living a life of great discipline and restraint. Without a doubt they have never spoken irresponsibly, never lied, did not easily promise something without ability to fulfill, did not make statements that they could not substantiate. They have used no craftiness; have not schemed or put on a mask to deceive people. They have shown no greed, have not unlawfully taken money or taken advantage of others; nor have they harmed others for personal gain. They have told no lewd stories but have been sober and discreet in their dealings with the opposite sex. They have been faithful to their mates. They have not furtively done things that could not be done before all. Whatever they have done has been done with consistency. They have not started something recklessly nor left things half done; were not fickle and inconstant, changing their mind to something new all the time. They have respected their parents, been kind to their brothers, concerned for their neighbors, merciful to their friends. They have worked hard and been faithful at their jobs. They have stood firmly at their post, neither aiming too high nor angling for praise or reputation. Everything has been done out in the open. They have spoken the truth and acted sincerely.

Because their actions were aboveboard these people may have suffered personal loss and been misunderstood, but their aim was to please God—always fearing God in their hearts with no concern for how difficult it might be. They just went ahead and did what they perceived to be the truth. God, in His turn, likewise did not let them down, because of their faithfulness and obedience. Consequently they were pleasing not only to Him but also gained the respect and love of others. Certainly lives like this continue to manifest the truth of the Bible and prove that its principles do not change: ". . . for whatever a man sows, this he will also reap."[4]

Background verses used in the above text:
1. Genesis 47:29-31, 49:28-33, 50:1-14
2. Genesis 50:24-26
3. Exodus 12:33,34,39
4. Galatians 6:7
5. Luke 6:38

十五

兩個自殺的人

15

Two Suicides

> *What does it profit a man to gain the whole world, and forfeit his soul? For what shall a man give in exchange for his soul?* —Mark 8:36,37.

Two sober examples are set before us in Scripture: In the Old Testament, there was an Ahithophel who hanged himself; in the New Testament, there was a Judas who hanged himself. Their manner of death was the same and their treachery was also the same.

Both these men were traitors who sold their masters and betrayed their friends. Ahithophel rebelled against his king, David; Judas sold his Lord, Jesus, to the enemy. The motive of each man was profit for himself; and as a consequence each gained nothing but met with a most pitiful and shameful end. God knows that whoever belongs to Him will meet such temptations, and that no matter who we are, we are still capable of committing such sins. But God is not willing that we should take the same disastrous road. Therefore He specifically, through His recorded Word, written by His servants, has seen to it that we have these sober examples in the Old Testament and the New Testament set before us in detail. Let us carefully study each episode.

Ahithophel was David's counselor.[1] He should have been loyal to David, assisting him in the time of peace and defending him in the time of crisis. When he heard that David's son, Absolom, was conspiring against the king, he should have tried his best to admonish the son to stop, warning him with righteous words and exposing the consequences of his proposed actions. If Absolom would not accept his warnings, he should at least not have become a party to Absolom's crime. Who could imagine that he would ever accede to the schemes of the rebellious son and feed him increasingly treacherous plans for fighting against his own father? How abominable were the two deadly strategies he offered Absolom!

The first item of advice Ahithophel gave was that Absolom should have sexual relations with his father's concubines in view of the public. This was suggested so that the people would consider David insulted beyond the possibility of reconciliation. Since David was the father and Absolom the son, if the son had a relationship with his father's concubine, that was a heinous sin, abhorrent and shameful. For one who had long been a close advisor to the king to have offered such an abominable strategy to the son of the king was to act like a beast in human garb. Even to read this account makes one boil with anger.

The second strategy was even more vicious. He advised Absolom to kill David and the sooner the better, even volunteering to personally lead twelve thousand men to chase down David at night and take his life. Imagine! He rebelled against his own king, he advised the son to kill his father, and he was willing to kill David himself. This was insidious, cruel, malicious and lacking in compassion! We can hardly believe that there could be a person who would plot such deeds!

Why did Ahithophel act in such a manner? Without a doubt he was trying to earn himself some credit in Absolom's sight that would stand him in good stead in the future, so that he might bask in Absolom's favor and occupy a high position in his court after he became king. He had visions of wielding great authority, probably in a high-salaried position, and enjoying life to the full.

If David had been a wicked despot without principle and his actions harmful to his country and people, we might be able to reason that Ahithophel was motivated to do these things for the sake of saving the Israelites from danger. Then he might have been able to justify killing David in order to save the country. But not only was David *not* a wicked despot, he was a *wise* and *good* king. Throughout his life, except for the Bathsheba episode and his shameful killing of Uriah, all that he had done before God commended him to be called "a man after God's own heart." The Bible records: "...David did what was right in the sight of the Lord, and had not turned aside from anything that He commanded him all the days of his life, except in the case of Uriah the Hittite."[2] Ahithophel was unquestionably attacking a wise and good king. He must have had a wicked heart to plot such cruel acts. If it were not for the sake of his own gain, what other motive could he have had?

From a person with a selfish heart, any terrible act can emerge. Anyone looking for selfish gain can lie, cheat, practice evil and plot for his self-interest. Anyone looking for selfish gain can disobey his parents and regard his brothers with enmity. Anyone looking for selfish gain can harm his spouse and befriend thieves. The majority of sins in this world issue from people who are out for selfish gain. They ruin others in order to pursue their own benefit. But a righteous God will not allow them to get away with it. They end up not in harming the other party but in harming themselves. So it was with Ahithophel.

Yes, Ahithophel rebelled against David and courted Absolom's favor, but suddenly he saw that Absolom was not intending to carry out the advice and strategy which he had recommended but was inclined to follow the counsel of Hushai the Archite.[3] Now he felt discredited and caught in a hard place, unable either to advance or retreat. He had lost his chance of getting rid of David and knew that ultimately Absolom would be defeated. When that should happen, he would no longer be able to face David because of his treachery. He would be subject to the harsh judgment of David against him. He could imagine how great would be his disgrace and punishment. Since eventually that would be awaiting him, he decided it would be better to take his own life now and end it all. So Ahithophel returned to his own city, set his house in order, and hanged himself.[4]

The road that Judas Iscariot took was similar to that of Ahithophel. For his own gain he sold his most gracious and righteous Master, the one who for three years had invested His love and instruction on him. He even pretended to be so intimate with Jesus that he used kissing as a sign to deliver his Master to the enemy. Think how depraved his heart must have been! How grievous was Judas' sin! His heart was as cruel as Ahithophel's and his vicious actions were in the same category as Ahithophel's. The consequence, too, was the same as his. In the Old Testament it was Ahithophel who sold his lord and friend and hanged himself; in the New Testament it was Judas who sold his Lord and friend and hanged himself. Though far apart in time, yet they face each other in history. Both fell and brought disgrace upon themselves, and their infamy is recorded for all generations to come.

In the whole Bible there are only these two records of men who sold their masters and friends and hanged themselves. In the world today and in the church there are countless people selling their employers and friends. Words such as "loyalty," "gratitude," and "principle" have become outmoded; "compassion" and "friendship" have lost their value. People take advantage of and cheat and lie to each other. One is treated as a bosom friend when he can be made use of; if not, then suddenly he becomes a stranger. This is considered as acceptable behavior. One may be a good friend today and an enemy tomorrow. Today a man might be profitable to you; tomorrow he may be like a painful ulcer to you. Two men may work together for a few years and outwardly be friends, but actually they are constantly on the watch to deceive each other, each looking for an opportunity to harm the other. If they are equally cunning or evil, there will be a balance of power. But should one win and the other lose, under those circumstances we can't really say that either was treated unjustly. But the most pitiful situation is when one person is actually sincere but the other is hypocritical.

One regards the other as a trustworthy friend but the other regards him as one to be oppressed. One speaks sincerely to the other while the other is quietly plotting deceit. One is genuinely loyal and true to the other, while his "friend" is sharpening his sword. Consequently the sincere person suffers severely from the other, while the cunning person secretly claps his hands with glee, congratulating himself on his tricky schemes. We know that since a righteous, just and faithful God sees what is happening, will He not be angry and punish such a cruel and callous sinner?

No wonder many people fight against God, deny His very existence and try to tear down and blot out all knowledge of Him. Their own wicked deeds cause them to be afraid and uneasy under His watchful eye. If they don't do away with God, they know that God will do away with them. They do not realize that what they are attempting to do is just as foolish as a fragile locust trying to stop a chariot with its puny strength—as sensible as striking a stone with an egg. If they really want to escape God's punishment, the only way is to confess and repent of their sins. God has prepared salvation and forgiveness through Jesus our Saviour as the only way for sinners to come before God.

There are many vicious and cruel people in the world at large who sell their masters and friends. We do not need to document this. The most heartbreaking thing is that there are also such people found in the churches. Outwardly they are disciples of Christ; inwardly they are just like Judas Iscariot. They follow Jesus for their own gain. They may appear to lift up Jesus and even to preach Him. At the same time they can betray Jesus and sell Him to the enemy. Their attitude toward Jesus is measured by their own gain or loss. Such people are the enemies of Christ, just the same as those who fight against Jesus outside of the churches. Their hypocritical manner deceives many. They do not appear to oppose Jesus; indeed, they seem to show respect and love and support for Him. But they are just like Judas when he said to Jesus, "Hail, Rabbi!" and kissed Him.[5] Who would guess that while these people are similarly "kissing Jesus" they are delivering Him to the enemy?

When Judas sold his Lord he did not actually do damage to

his Lord, but on the contrary, he was a link to accomplish the work of salvation that God had already planned. For when the Lord Jesus drank the bitter cup of death, He was exalted on high with a name given Him which is above every name. The one most to be pitied was Judas himself. For him there was no way of escape. It was too late to repent. At that critical juncture he could only take the road of suicide. He ended his life with a rope.[6] After he hanged himself, he even fell down to the earth and "...he burst open in the middle and all his bowels gushed out."[7] In attempting to hurt others, he consequently hurt himself. In his attempt to sell the Lord, he lost his own life for nothing.

The hearts of people in the world are cruel and cunning, ungrateful, disloyal and treacherous. We have no way to stop those people nor any power to persuade them to stop their evil actions. But we, as Christians, should by no means follow in their footsteps. We should be upright, hiding nothing, sincere and honest and loyal before all men; willing to be deceived by others yet never deceiving them; never, for our own benefit, harming others. If anyone treats us with kindness and goodness, we should always be conscientious to repay him. We should honor our parents who have nurtured us, love our own kinsmen and brothers and sisters. We should each be faithful toward our spouse. Toward our masters and friends we should always be consistent. When they meet calamity or have special needs we should offer them our help, being especially sympathetic with them and standing loyally by their side. If we act like the people of this world, practicing disloyalty, unrighteousness and treachery, we fall into our own trap of self-seeking. Sooner or later we will end up like Ahithophel and Judas. Such a pity that would be!

What a sorrowful picture to visualize: A tree on the left with Ahithophel hanging from it—a wise man but full of scheming, ending up by falling into his own trap; and another tree on the right, from which hangs a broken rope and under which lies the traitor Judas, whose belly has burst from his fall. Whenever we are tempted to be disloyal and self-seeking, considering to sell out our benefactor or friend, let us hasten to visualize these two pitiful men who committed suicide.

Background verses used in the above text:

[1] 1 Chronicles 27:33;
2 Samuel 15:12, 16:15,20-23
[2] 1 Kings 15:4,5
[3] 2 Samuel 17:1-14
[4] 2 Samuel 17:23
[5] Matthew 26:14-16, 47-50
[6] Matthew 27:3-5
[7] Acts 1:18

十六

爲何懼怕恐嚇？

16

Why Fear Threats?

> God has not given us a spirit of timidity, but of power and love and discipline —2 Timothy 1:7.

After the Lord ascended into heaven, His disciples, having actually seen their resurrected Lord with their own eyes, were filled with the Holy Spirit and witnessed with power and authority. Therefore, it was reported throughout Jerusalem.[1] On the day of Pentecost about three thousand people repented and believed in the Lord, were baptized and entered into the ranks of the disciples. Not long after, Peter and John performed a miracle in Jesus' name: a man born lame was healed. He actually got up and walked. This miracle gained the attention of many people and they gathered around excitedly to watch. Peter took this opportunity to witness to them about the resurrection. When this came to the ears of the Jewish leaders, it made them panic. After Jesus' resurrection they had bribed the soldiers who watched

Jesus' tomb, instructing them to report that while they were sleeping the disciples stole His body.[2] Now, to the surprise of the Jewish leaders, from the day of Pentecost the apostles began to proclaim Jesus' resurrection with great power, boldly, out in the open.

When Peter and John performed the above miracle, they made it a point to say that they did so in the name of the resurrected Jesus. In this way, they not only witnessed to Jesus' resurrection by their words but used the fact of the miracle to prove Jesus' resurrection. This way of witnessing was very effective and convinced many to believe in Jesus. This was just what the Jewish leaders could not tolerate. Therefore an unfortunate incident occured: the leaders "laid hands on them and put them in jail until the next day...."[3]

Now that they had Peter and John in prison, they really didn't know how to deal with them and hoped that by the next day they could come up with a good strategy. They began by cross-examining them in the presence of many important and influential leaders.[4] The scene was just like ferocious lions surrounding two innocent rabbits to attack them. These two apostles, humble fishermen by trade, surely had never before been in such an imposing setting. Humanly speaking, they should have been terrified and trembling, unable to utter a word, only falling to the ground and pleading for mercy before such men of authority and power. In the natural, we would expect them to promise never again to preach the resurrection. If they could only avoid a sentence—whew, they would be getting off easy!

Was that the case? No, absolutely not! Peter was filled with the Holy Spirit and witnessed before all those Jewish dignitaries. He made a point of declaring, "[This healing was] by the name of Jesus Christ, the Nazarene, whom *you* crucified...." This statement was the same as if sentence was passed on *their* sin, declaring that they had rebelled against God and resisted God because they crucified Jesus—"whom *God* raised from the dead." He continued by declaring, "He is the stone which was rejected by you, the builders, but which became the very cornerstone."[5] This allusion to Scripture not only underscored the sinfulness of their deed but also thoroughly disgraced them. Finally Peter spoke out that great and precious truth: "And there is salvation in no one else; for there is no other name under heaven that has been given among men, by which we must be saved."[6] These words explained that the Jesus whom they had crucified had fulfilled God's plan by becoming the Saviour of the world. These words exalted Christ whom *God* exalted, and were also God's reproof to the hardhearted Jews.

I would imagine that those "rulers, elders and scribes, Annas the high priest, Caiaphas and John and Alexander," who were now smarting greatly, were upset and angry enough to immediately have taken Peter and John outside the city and stoned them to death. Unexpectedly, they didn't do that. What did they do? They observed the apostles' confidence—that in spite of being uneducated men, they seemed fearless. So they called a private conference to decide what strategy they should employ against them. Truly amazing! These influential, important Jews, with complete authority in their hands to arraign these two simple men, were actually rebuked by them. They apparently did not lose their tempers but rather marveled because of the courage of the two and "recognized them as having been with Jesus, and . . . had nothing to reply."

These Jewish leaders now had seen two wonders: one, a man born lame who stood up and walked; the other, two untrained men who expressed remarkable power and courage in witnessing boldly to the resurrection of Jesus. They could not help but marvel and were hard put as to how they should deal with them. When they had arrested them the day before and put them in prison, they knew that the next day they would have to seriously decide how to deal with them. Who would have guessed that they would have had no recourse or way out?

Things had already developed to such a point that, since they had the two already in custody, they were forced to find a way to resolve the matter. So they called for a closed session, ordering Peter and John out of the Council chamber so that only their own people were present.

How to deal with such a touchy matter? They concluded that they could not deny the recent miracle because all who lived in Jerusalem knew about it. So they had no recourse but to choose a pitifully mild and empty way to deal with them: "Let us warn them to speak no more to any man in this name." Moreover, they could not keep Peter and John in prison without pressing further charges. Certainly they could not stone them to death, because they had not committed any crime against the law. The only crime they could put their finger on was that they created rumors to confuse people, preaching that Jesus was alive. But now that the born-lame beggar had been healed in Jesus' name and was actually walking around, people would naturally conclude that Jesus really had risen. Under such circumstances they could find no crime of which to accuse the apostles; consequently there was no sentence to pass on them, no way to punish them or deal harshly with them. They had *no way out*, yet they *had* to find a way out—their conclusion: to threaten them!

So they executed their decision and "commanded them not to speak or teach at all in the name of Jesus." What was the response of the two? Peter and John said, "Whether it is right in the sight of God to give heed to you rather than to God, you be the judge; for we cannot stop speaking what we have seen and heard."[7] Although threatening is really meaningless and a weak action, yet it is very effective against certain people who are afraid of threats. If applied against those who are not afraid, it is utterly ineffective. Even if those with great authority do the threatening, courageous people do not recant. Because these two valiant men were not afraid of threats, they were entirely unaffected by them. Because the Jewish leaders were in a corner, they resorted to this ineffective way of escape. After that, they released them, having gotten nowhere with their threatening.

Although Peter and John were filled with the Holy Spirit, speaking with great boldness and without fear of the threats of the Jews, the rest of the believers may have been quite fearful. Therefore when Peter and John were released, they went back to report the victory to their brethren. After they heard the full story and were encouraged, they called upon God with one accord with great joy. In their prayer they also mentioned the threat of the Jews: "And now, Lord, take note of their threats, and grant that Thy bond-servants may speak Thy word with all confidence."[8] When they finished their praying, God immediately answered it—in that "the place where they had gathered together was shaken, and they were all filled with the Holy Spirit, and began to speak the word of God with boldness."[9]

That morning there may have been only two people filled with the Spirit and not afraid of threats. By evening there were many people filled with the Holy Spirit and also not afraid of threats. The gospel was widely spread abroad under such circumstances. The church expanded. The gospel could now reach out to the whole world, and we, in our turn, can have the wonderful opportunity to hear and accept God's salvation too! All of this was because of the example of those who were not afraid of threats. If the apostles and those with them had been afraid of the threats of the Jews, then they would not have dared to preach and teach in Jesus' name. Where then would the church be today?

Let us notice what purpose the Jews had in threatening the disciples. The Jews knew that the apostles and those with them were deeply rooted in their faith in Jesus. They were unmovable. So they gave up trying to make them *renounce* their faith. But they thought that if they could just stop them from *preaching Jesus*, no more new converts would join the church. Those who already believed in Jesus would gradually become weak or scattered and eventually die out. After ten or twenty years the followers of Christ would disappear from the nation of the Jews. The authorities couldn't do much to change those who *already* believed in Jesus, but they thought they could at least cause them to cease preaching Jesus by threatening them. To their surprise, the disciples were not at all afraid of threats; on the contrary, they preached with even more boldness. The strategy the Jews used completely failed and the gospel of Christ was victorious!

Ever since that time, wherever the gospel of Christ is preached it meets opposition; at the same time, there are always people accepting it, whatever the consequences, and becoming Christians. The greatest hope of those who opposed Christ was that believers would rebel against Christ and believe in Him no longer. But, should this hope fail, at least they might retreat for a while and stop preaching Christ. In that way, no more people would turn to Christ. And when Christians stopped increasing, the gospel of Christ would gradually die out of its own accord.

Though there might be many ways to suppress Christians and keep them from preaching Christ, the leaders figured that the safest and easiest way was simply to threaten. If they used more drastic measures, it might bring the matter to public attention and cause a bad reaction. Another great concern to them was that the more they persecuted the sincere Christians, the stronger they might become in their faith. To use drastic measures against them would be equal to encouraging the progress of their faith. Having such concern, those that were more far-sighted and more thoughtful would not advocate harsh ways to oppose the gospel, but relied on threatening. If this reaped a good result, they would be happy; if not, it would not be too difficult for them to try another direction.

Has this strategy of threatening really reaped any results? Though it certainly had no effect in the days of the apostles, unfortunately it has had great effectiveness in the church in later generations.

One reason is that the church of later generations has lost the firm and pure faith of the apostles. Christians are not out and out, not firmly convinced of the power of the resurrected Christ, not fervently looking for the return of Christ. Therefore many believers love the world, are careless and take their ease. Another reason is that the church lacks courageous, firm and faithful leaders who serve the Lord in spite of being threatened from the outside. Because the leaders are afraid, first they fail and fall; then other believers, looking to them as examples, do not stand firm in the faith either.

Still another reason is that the members of the church are a mixed group. Many without genuine faith or eternal life join the visible church. Some of them even become leaders of the church. If they have no pure spiritual motive for joining the church, they just blindly join. So when they meet any threats, they naturally and immediately surrender to the world. Not content to stop there, they may turn right around and attack the church and sell out the Saviour, seriously hurting the brethren. Under such circumstances, and for that kind of people, threatening is indeed a most effective way to dissipate the church.

Being afraid of threats and not daring to preach the gospel any longer is heartbreaking enough. But worse, some believers who are afraid of threats even deny their Lord and dare not obey the command of God nor speak truth, but fear attack and persecution. Actually, those who use verbal threats rarely have any real intentions of attacking and persecuting them. Their tactic is only to frighten people, using this mild and easy way to make them surrender. These pitiful believers would be scared off just by hearing frightening voices. How lamentable! If they would just hold their ground, they would find that no real danger would befall them. Being struck down is shameful, but to be "threatened down" is much, much more shameful!

There's another thing to notice. When the apostles and those with them bore testimony for the Lord with firmness and boldness, they were filled with the Holy Spirit. "Peter was filled with the Holy Spirit and said to them..."; "...when they had prayed, the place where they had gathered together was shaken, and they were all filled with the Holy Spirit, and began to speak the word of God with boldness."[9] Yes, only the one who is filled with the Holy Spirit has this superhuman boldness and power and is not afraid of any threat. He does not try to avoid any danger but goes right on bravely testifying for his Lord. At the same time, this boldness and power was also the manifestation of the filling of the Holy Spirit. A believer who claims to be filled with the Holy Spirit but appears to be frightened and without power is deceiving others and being deceived himself. A believer having the experience of the filling of the Holy Spirit does not need to testify with his mouth to that fact but can let his actions speak for themselves. No place in the Bible is it recorded that a disciple declared with his own mouth that he was filled with the Holy Spirit. However, the Bible does record the testimonies of those who saw the results of the filling of the Holy Spirit.[10]

The Scriptures show us the truth that only those who have a lifestyle pleasing to God are filled with the Holy Spirit. It is they who, when special needs or labors arise, have power, authority, boldness and wisdom to meet those needs and tasks. We ourselves may not feel that we are filled with the Spirit, but others can see that we are. Then we will have the same victorious experience as the apostles when we are threatened.

After Jesus' ascension into heaven the gospel spread everywhere in spite of hardships and persecution, because the disciples were not afraid of threats even from the first encounter with them in Jerusalem. If there were disciples of such caliber in the church today, men and women unmoved by threats, who then could stop the gospel from being spread through all the earth?

Background verses used in the above text:

1. Acts 4:1-31
2. Matthew 28:11-15
3. Acts 4:1-3
4. Acts 4:4-12
5. Acts 4:11
6. Acts 4:12
7. Acts 4:19,20
8. Acts 4:29,30
9. Acts 4:31
10. Acts 2:1-4, 7:54-56, 13:6-12

十七

為何抓住生命？

17

Why Hang On to Life?

> *I am convinced that neither death, nor life, nor angels, nor principalities, nor things present, nor things to come, nor powers, nor height, nor depth, nor any other created thing, shall be able to separate us from the love of God, which is in Christ Jesus our Lord* —Romans 8:38,39.

The apostle Paul was truly a faithful and courageous servant of God. He not only did not seek his own gain, fame or honor, he did not even regard his life as precious.[1] Because he was not greedy, he could afford to be fearless and not cowardly in speaking out the whole counsel of God. No wonder God greatly used him and the word of God through him was so powerful.

    To be a good servant of God is truly not an easy matter. God loves people and desires that they be blessed. He shows people the way to receive His blessings. How regrettable that people are so foolish as to not walk in God's way but rather do as they please, ultimately bringing trouble on themselves. Because God loves them, He raises up His servants and speaks to the people through them. On one hand He rebukes their sin, drawing them to repentance; on the other hand, He points out to them the way in which He wants them to walk. If people are thinking clearly, by all means they should receive God's message and thank His servant whom He has sent to proclaim it. But the majority of people have their minds clouded by sin. Their thoughts are confused, literally upside down. Not only don't they receive God's word, but they openly oppose it. Under such circumstances, those who speak for God become objects of attack.

It would be no surprise if the opposition came only from idolaters and infidels, but unfortunately it also comes from God's people. The Israelites opposed God by persecuting the prophets of old who spoke for God. Scripture bears record to this.[2] The words which God spoke when commissioning certain of the prophets also prove this fact.[3] If we carefully read the Bible, we will see that the prophets who spoke for God always suffered much persecution and attack.

Since speaking for God turns out to be so hard and dangerous, the one who works for God must have strong motivation; otherwise he could not be faithful to God and would not dare speak forth what God wanted him to say, without discounting any of God's truth. If a servant of God is continually anxious about his own life and reputation, he will never be greatly used by God and will certainly not have power in his ministry. Not many will be converted through him nor benefit from his message. A fearful person is not qualified to work for God. Paul was not like that. Since he desired nothing upon earth, he was not afraid of anything either. He didn't covet money, comfort, pleasure, honor; nor did he value his own life. Because of that, Satan could not use the profit motive to tempt him or bring him into any danger. Such things had lost their hold on Paul and so were not effective to deter him. He could be faithful and obedient and fulfill all the commission God had given him.

Before the elders at Ephesus, Paul stated, "I do not consider my life of any account as dear to myself."[4] Some people might wonder if Paul was not boasting. If he confronted some really dangerous situation, would he actually practice what he preached? Let us look at the record. When Agabus came down from Judea, he conveyed the word of the Holy Spirit that the Jews at Jerusalem would bind Paul and deliver him into the hands of the Gentiles. When the believers heard that, they begged Paul with weeping not to go up to Jerusalem. What was his response? He said, "What are you doing, weeping and breaking my heart? For I am ready not only to be bound, but even to die at Jerusalem for the name of the Lord Jesus."[5]

I am not surprised that the believers carried on that way, trying to stop Paul after hearing the prophecy of Agabus. It might have reminded some of them of the time that Jesus Himself set His face steadfastly toward Jerusalem, knowing what awaited Him there—that He would be delivered to the priests and scribes and thereafter to the Gentiles, to be put to death. With that in their memories, they could easily deduce that this time Paul would meet the same sort of fate as his Lord. Therefore they wept and tried to hold him back. Paul was probably aware of the same possibility. If he could have been tempted by love for his own life, then even if there had been no believers to stop him, he would have canceled the idea of going to Jerusalem. And how much more would he have been ready to yield to their pleading. After reading of this incident, we can certainly affirm that Paul was an apostle who did not care for his life.

Not only did Paul himself speak in this manner, others also witnessed this about him. In fact, the apostles and elders of the church at Jerusalem had already testified about both Paul and Barnabas that they "...risked their lives for the name of our Lord Jesus Christ."[6] This is enough to prove that neither Paul nor his co-workers counted their lives of any value. Since the church in apostolic times had such exemplary leaders, no wonder the church was courageous, strong, active, powerful and effective, though it faced great opposition.

Today, many servants of God preach only to earn their own livelihood. How many will ignore their own gain or loss, glory or disgrace, safety or danger, life or death, and only seek to be faithful to God? Not many. Not only are the majority of preachers narrow-minded, but so is their outlook when it comes to risking their lives for the Lord. Yes, they want to work for God but at the same time they desire to taste the pleasures of this world. Therefore they end up as men-pleasers, hoping to gain some profit or honor by bowing low before others. Would you expect that such preachers would risk their lives for the gospel? That is hardly likely. Their way of thinking and lifestyle causes them to be afraid of death and cling to life, drifting along with the world's idea. Consequently, God cannot use them and the glory of God cannot be manifested in their lives.

We read in the book of Daniel how God manifested His great power and glory through the three young Hebrew men and Daniel. Was it not because these men were faithful to God regardless of anything, gladly risking their lives? If they had been afraid of death and clung to life, they would have worshiped the golden image. Could God then have manifested His power through the miracle of delivering them from the blazing furnace? If Daniel had considered clinging to his life and ceasing from his daily habit of praying three times, would God have sent angels to seal the lions' mouths? The God of the saints of old is also our God. Today we seldom see the glory of God and experience such wonderful results as they had because we love our selves and our lives. What great loss we suffer! How foolish we are! Not only should the *servants of God* not count their lives dear, but the same attitude should be expressed in *every* Christian in order to be victorious. We should *all* have such determination before God and men.

From the first coming of the Lord Jesus into the world until He comes again, everyone who would faithfully follow Him must pass through adversity, distress, attacks and persecution. One should not expect to be a Christian and escape adversity and distress. If we are afraid of anything at all, Satan will use that particular fear to threaten and defeat us. Through our own cowardice we will fall and fail. If we have nothing to long for on earth—neither wealth, pleasure, honor, gain, nor our very lives—Satan will absolutely have no power over us. We will not only be victorious but more than conquerors through our Lord Jesus who loved us.[7]

Actually it is not that difficult for Christians to let go of life on this earth. If we are persuaded that from the day we truly repented and believed in the Lord we received eternal life and will never die, then fear of death should not threaten us or control us. Our body may die, but the life we have received from the Lord is eternal. Therefore the Bible calls the death of saints "sleep." After our bodies sleep, our spirit leaves the body and goes to be with the Lord.[8] From the

Why Hang On to Life?

Bible record we know that those who leave this world have their spirits received by the Lord to be ever with Him. The body sleeps until the glorified Lord descends from heaven; then the body will rise from the grave and will be changed, together with the bodies of the saints who are still alive, and then they all will be with Him forever.[9] For these reasons, Christians should not cling to their earthly lives or be afraid of death. Not that they are indifferent, paying no attention to death, but that they know the Lord tasted death for them already and overcame its power. He gives this same victory to those who sincerely trust His name. They know that they cannot die, so they can be fearless in life and in death, having a firm faith and hope. Released from this ultimate fear, they can live a victorious life on earth such as is beyond people's imaginings.

What a pity that many Christians, although they have received salvation and truly have eternal life, don't consider the facts of the Word of God and put their hope in the promises of God! They let the prestige and pleasures of this world fill their hearts and allow all sorts of worldly things to obscure their vision, so that they value the things of this world more than the things of heaven. They are always distressed in mind—frantically trying to get rich and then troubled and anxious lest they lose the riches. Eventually they suffer loss and God's name is disgraced.

Oh, we need a few more like Paul, who despised this world and longed for the Lord's return, not clinging to his life, but was motivated only by the desire to be faithful to God and lead many to walk in the path of victory!

- - - - - - -

Background verses used in the above text:

[1] Acts 20:17-24
[2] Matthew 5:12, 23:34
[3] Jeremiah 1:17-19; Ezekiel 2:3-7, 3:7-9
[4] Acts 20:24
[5] Acts 21:10-14
[6] Acts 15:22-26
[7] Romans 8:37
[8] Acts 7:59,60; Philippians 1:23
[9] 2 Corinthians 4:16,17; 1 Thessalonians 4:13-17; 1 Corinthians 15:50-57

十八

當基督站起來時

18

When Christ Stands Up

The Lord says to my Lord: "Sit at My right hand" —Psalm 110:1a.

He gazed intently into heaven and saw the glory of God, and Jesus standing at the right hand of God —Acts 7:55.

Perhaps over a thousand years before our Lord came to earth, David the Psalmist was moved by the Holy Spirit to prophesy that Christ would sit at the right hand of God. The apostles also testified that He was seated there after His resurrection. This matter is attested to by at least eleven references.[1] Therefore, the Lord Jesus Christ must be sitting at the right hand of God now.

Why then, just before Stephen was to give up his life as a martyr, did he see the Lord Jesus *standing* at the right hand of God? The record clearly states, "But being full of the Holy Spirit, he gazed intently into heaven and saw the glory of God, and Jesus standing at the right hand of God."[2] Actually then, is the Lord Jesus *standing* or *sitting* at the right hand of God? If the eleven references cited about Christ sitting are accurate, is this reference inaccurate? If this reference is trustworthy, then are the other references untrustworthy? And why should this incidental fact be worthy of our attention?

Both are accurate. How can this be? The majority references refer to the usual situation. The record in Acts is the situation on that special day when Stephen was about to be cruelly put to death by the Jews. The Lord had been sitting there since His ascension. But the faithful witness of Stephen for His name and His word had so enraged the Jews that they "gnashed their teeth at him" and were ready to put him to death. At that time, the Son of God who sits at God's right hand, in order to express respect and welcome to His faithful servant, stood up from where He was sitting. So when Stephen gazed up, he saw Jesus standing.

It is significant that when the disciples of Christ bravely witness for His name and His word, suffer humiliation and attack, persecution and death, even the Christ who sits at the right hand of God takes note and stands up from His seat, expressing respect and welcome to them. What a glorious thing to contemplate!

If one of us were to have the opportunity to meet a famous man who is honored here on earth, and when he sees us approaching we realize he has risen from his seat to express welcome and respect to us, one who is his inferior, how would we feel? Such a glorious honor! Now if God's very Son, who received the glory of God, and whom God has lifted up as the highest and given a name above every name— the One who became "the King of kings and Lord of lords"—if *He* stands up to welcome a disciple who has suffered for His name's sake, how many times more glorious that is when compared to the respect shown us by any man of this earth?

All people of this world must die sooner or later. Some die ordinary deaths, others die by some accident. The majority die from disease, sickness, starvation, in floods, war, or some accident on land, sea or in the air. Sometimes people are crushed by collapsing buildings, struck by lightning, suffer accidental poisoning, are bitten by venomous snakes or attacked by wild beasts. Some people die by suicide, are victims of arson, or having committed serious crimes are put to death by the courts. Rather than any of these, the most ideal death is to die at a ripe old age without sickness. Among the ways of death, this way is thought to be the best and is the most desired by many. Therefore in Peking we call the funeral of an aged person a "happy funeral."

But in the eyes of Christians, nothing can compare with being put to death for the sake of our Lord's name and word—which is much more beautiful, glorious and admirable. It is this kind of death which can cause Christ to stand up at the right hand of God and express respect and welcome. Moreover, there are special promises to such persons: "...be faithful until death, and I will give you the crown of life."[3] Yes, those who give up their lives for this reason, at the return of the Lord will also receive the crown of life which the Lord especially prepared for them. This is not a crown for ordinary Christians. After fully grasping this truth, we will perceive that in the eyes of Christians the most glorious, admirable death is not to die of ripe old age without sickness, but to lose one's life for the sake of the Lord's name and word. If a Christian can die like this it is surely God's special mercy, because this kind of blessing is not easy to attain.

We read in the history of the church about believers of old who were killed for the Lord's name by those idol-worshiping kings and officials and mobs who were aroused to high frenzy to oppose God's people. Those believers were willing to choose the way of bloodshed and never rebelled against the God they trusted. When one fell, others took up the banner, counting it an honor to die for a righteous cause, looking at death as going home. They could only have been so brave because they had the full assurance that this kind of death was glorious and admirable. Others might consider that it was loss, but it was in reality their greatest gain and blessing. Unfortunately, early in the fourth century, the gospel of Christ was made a tool of the Roman emperor and consequently church and politics became mixed together. The word of God was adulterated and has been for the past thousand-some years since. So today, what many preachers preach and what many church members believe is unfortunately not the pure gospel of the Lord Jesus and not what His apostles preached.

In certain instances there has been an abnormal growth in the church, adding many nominal Christians—the majority of whom do not have either true faith or eternal life. Because of such a situation, the majority of "Christians" do not possess the attitude of looking at death as going home but are timid and cringing, afraid of death and clinging to life. Anxious, carelessly passing the time, not daring to resist sin, they are ashamed to confess the Lord's name under adverse circumstances. Not even upholding their own faith, they shamelessly sell out their Lord. Distorting the gospel, they hope to gain a bit of good will through association with God's people, but at the same time hope to avoid persecution and calamity. Such people will not only be cast away by the Lord, but in the end even the infidels will look down on them, despising them, considering them not worth a cent. It causes much harm to have such people in the church because even some who originally had the true faith and life are influenced for evil by them, follow them, and become weak in their faith. As our Lord looks at this lamentable situation, how His heart must ache and break!

In such grievous and painful circumstances, we need to ask God to raise up valiant men who are faithful to the Lord, pointing the way for the rest of believers, walking boldly in the path the saints of the Lord and His apostles have trod. Strong and courageous, fearing no danger, who do "not love their life even to death"[4] but step bravely toward it, considering it an honor to bear disgrace for the sake of the Lord's name—that is the kind of men the church needs! Men should be fighting to give up their lives for the Lord like athletes compete for medals on the playing field. "Virtue does not stand alone; it will attract neighbors," according to the Chinese proverb. It requires only one person to take such a stand and consequently many others are encouraged, influenced by them, and God's name will be glorified. The power of the resurrection of Christ will then be shown forth. This unbelieving generation will see the manifestation of God's power through such valiant men. They will also be respected and welcomed by our Lord. In the day of His glorious appearing, they will receive the incorruptible crown which was promised to such men.

Maybe some will ask, "If I could only have the opportunity to give my life for the Lord, that would be my highest choice; but if in my whole lifetime I do not have such a chance, then would I be most unfortunate?"

It is easy to answer that. Certainly, comparatively speaking, not many believers actually have the opportunity of martyrdom, yet every Christian can be like these valiant, victorious men. We need only have the same faith, courage, determination and a *ready attitude* to give our lives for the Lord, under any circumstances. We ought not to be afraid, nor drift along with the current, nor sell out the Lord, nor disgrace the Lord's name, disobey His commands, or disappoint Him in His expectation of us. Then, even if we do not have the opportunity actually to be martyrs, we can receive the glory and reward of the saints who did so.[5] This is true because what the Lord wants of us is a heart and attitude of faithfulness to Him. We can still have an experience like Stephen, being welcomed and honored by the Lord. On the other hand, if a believer fears dangers and surrenders to the world, but then the world kills him anyway because he has followed Jesus, I do not think that person would be counted as having *given* his life for the Lord. Rather, his life has been *taken* from him. I doubt if he will receive that special reward reserved for the faithful disciples.

If we fully understand this truth, we will not worry or give much thought to whether we will actually have the opportunity of giving our lives for the Lord. All we need is the *willingness* and the *determination* and *faithfulness* to do so.

Though there are numerous ways Satan can attack us, there are basically two categories: first, by temptations; second, by threats. The former includes temptation to money, pleasure, fame, friendships, love, etc. The latter includes insults, contempt, loss of employment, poverty, loneliness, imprisonment, calamity, death, etc. Among these latter, death is considered by most of mankind to be the most serious and fearful thing because of its finality. Fear of death and the clinging to life is the common feeling of everyone. Christians are also human. Naturally they will also fear death and hang on to life. Satan will use this weak point of Christians to attack them and they will most certainly reap the result. Because many Christians fear death, they are defeated at Satan's feet.

If we all understand that to give our lives for the name of the Lord is not loss but gain, not a thing to be afraid of but a thing to be desired and for which to be congratulated, we won't be moved by fear of death. Satan's final device will be rendered ineffective.[6] Thus, not only will we be victorious, but "in all these things we [will] overwhelmingly conquer through Him who loved us."[7]

- - - - - - -

Background verses used in the above text:

[1] Psalm 110:1;
  Matthew 22:41-46, 26:64;
  Luke 22:66-69;
  Acts 2:34;
  Ephesians 1:19-21;
  Colossians 3:1;
  Hebrews 1:1-3, 8:1,2, 10:12,13, 12:1,2
[2] Acts 7:55,56
[3] Revelation 2:10
[4] Revelation 12:10,11
[5] James 1:12
[6] 1 Corinthians 15:55-57
[7] Romans 8:35-39

十九

警惕鬆弦了

19

Relaxing Your Vigilance

> *Be on the alert. Your adversary, the devil, prowls about like a roaring lion, seeking someone to devour. But resist him, firm in your faith* —1 Peter 5:8b,9a.

When David was fleeing from Absolom, a man named Shimei reviled and cursed David. So when Solomon succeeded his father David as king, he restricted Shimei and warned him to live only in Jerusalem, prohibiting him from traveling to any other place. He was warned that if he ever crossed over the brook Kidron, "...you will know for certain that you shall surely die."[1] When Shimei heard this, he answered Solomon, "The word is good. As my lord the king has said, so your servant will do."

We can imagine that after Shimei heard this stern warning he must have trembled with fear and dared not leave Jerusalem even a single step. He remembered the miserable and shameful fact that he had cursed the king. He also knew that Solomon would be watching for the opportunity to make him pay for his sin. Since he obviously loved his life, he dared not go beyond Solomon's prohibition lest he bring trouble and death down upon his head.

So then, what a surprise! After only three years of obedience he actually dared to leave Jerusalem and go to Gath to find his two runaway servants—and brought on what he knew full well could be his death sentence. Solomon had given him such a severe warning that even after thirty years he should not have forgotten it. How could he have forgotten in such a short time? No, he probably did not forget that warning but, instead, just took it lightly. He had lived in peace for three years in Jerusalem and Solomon neither bothered him nor repeated his prohibition. His sense of fear began to diminish as the months went by. He may have thought that since nothing had happened during such a long period, nor had he encountered any danger, why should he spend the rest of his days in fear and trembling and unnecessary restriction? He may have felt more and more relieved as the months went by. His life became more comfortable. Gradually he felt an unconcern toward King Solomon's prohibition. He conjectured that the days of danger must be past. Solomon's warning had lost its edge for him. Because he yielded to this kind of thinking, he dared ignore the limitations put upon him. Consequently he lost his life.

We can imagine how remorseful he must have felt just before his life was taken. Had it really been worth it? How he must have hated himself for being so careless and foolhardy, falling into this self-made trap because of wrong thinking. But what was the use of regret and self-condemnation at that point? If he had kept a wary and watchful heart from the beginning to the end, he would not have considered transgressing Solomon's command even if *three times* three years had passed without any incident.

A similar lot has befallen many, and for the same reasons. In the beginning they may have known about some danger, so with a wary and watchful heart, day and night they dared not be heedless or careless. Because they paid attention to the situation and were alert, they escaped danger. But as the days dragged on, they felt they were safe and that no more danger would come upon them. They slipped into carelessness

Relaxing Your Vigilance 143

and let their guard down. Suddenly, when they thought all was peace and safety, calamity struck.

A certain woman who had been almost fatally ill had begun to recover after being treated by a doctor. The doctor strictly warned her about certain things she should not do and things she should not eat—or else, were this condition to reoccur, her life would be in danger. After she received the doctor's warning she was extremely vigilant day and night, paying attention every moment and not forgetting the doctor's orders. But after a year or two, during which time she had suffered no relapse, gradually she began to neglect her vigilance and proceeded to do what the doctor had ordered her not to do and to eat what the doctor had prohibited her from eating. She became seriously ill again. Certainly she regretted that she had disobeyed the doctor's orders, but it was too late. The illness claimed her life.

A certain captain was commissioned by his general to lead his troops in defending a key sector. The general warned him, "The enemy is very tricky and may strike at odd times. Be on the alert day and night; never for a moment neglect your vigilance. If you fail, the whole army will be in jeopardy." This captain knew the reputation of his experienced and wise commander, so he ordered the soldiers under him to watchfully defend the position day and night. One week passed, then two weeks, three weeks, a month, two months and three months. The enemy never sent out any major offensive unit against them. Sporadic skirmishes occurred involving only ten or twenty soldiers—just minor harassments and quick retreats. As the days went by, this captain became slack in his vigilance toward the enemy, considering that there was really no great threat and therefore no need to maintain full alert. He was no longer as watchful as before. The soldiers under him also grew less cautious. Then, without warning, after they had let down their guard, the enemy attacked with great force. Since they were not fully prepared to defend themselves they had no way to handle the onslaught and the whole army was annihilated in less than a day.

When a certain man set off on a journey of some distance that required passing through mountains and desert, his experienced friend told him that there would be wild beasts on this route and he had better take companions along with him for protection. He accepted his friend's warning, and each time he traveled with three or four comrades. But after journeying that way ten or twenty times and never encountering any wild beasts, he became more daring. He concluded that it was a safe journey after all, so why bother with taking companions? He embarked alone the next time, and as he entered the mountain pass he was attacked by a leopard. Because he was alone and defenceless, he became a feast for the beast.

Throughout history there are records of many who, prior to achieving success, were careful and cautious in many things; thus they met with great success. Afterward, however, they gradually became haughty and proud, thinking that there was nothing too hard for them. In time they threw caution to the winds and did whatever they pleased. While they were feeling safe and proud of themselves, they suddenly met with unexpected failure. Certainly they regretted their actions; they even hated themselves. But to no avail.

A scholar of the Sung dynasty said: "Matters in this world are accomplished through caution and fail through negligence. Watchfulness is the source of blessing; negligence is the gateway to calamity." This is truly a golden precept. Anyone, in whatever circumstances, can, with proper caution, avoid many dangers and calamities; but with an attitude of negligence and taking warnings lightly, they may—even if there is no direct danger—bring calamity on themselves.

When Solomon had Shimei killed, he must have sighed about Shimei's foolhardiness. He might have sat in his palace later that day and mused. *What a foolish man you were, Shimei! You knew for sure you would be killed when you left Jerusalem. You yourself said to me, "This saying is good; even as my lord the king has said, your servant will do." Why did you become so daring, throwing your life away?*

Being the wisest man, Solomon saw what had happened to Shimei and could not have missed the lesson it taught. But after a number of years, the king himself took the same route as Shimei. When he had finished building both the temple and the palace, the Lord appeared to him and told him that if he served God with all his heart and feared Him, He would bless him; but if he or his sons observed not the statutes of God and turned away to worship other gods, He would abandon them and let the temple be destroyed.[2] As Solomon heard these words he surely must have trembled with holy fear and determined in his heart always to act cautiously, fearful lest he depart from the Lord and meet calamity. Who could have imagined that after a number of years Solomon would follow the heathen women whom he loved and begin to worship their manifold false gods, thus inviting God's severe curse?[3] Shimei was killed by Solomon, but Solomon himself took the same path.

Seeing others fail and suffer doom, feeling sorry for them and bemoaning their fate, is not difficult. Seeing others fail and experience the consequences is one thing. But taking it as a personal warning for oneself and never forgetting it, so that one does not follow the same disastrous road, is a much harder thing. Even such a wise person as Solomon was not able to avoid that pitfall; much less many people who are not as wise as he!

Are believers today able to avoid the disastrous road that Shimei and Solomon took? Certainly, and the way to do it is simple. One must always have a watchful heart. In whatever state you find yourself, don't think that the ground is firm under you and that you yourself could never fall. Do not neglect the warnings and commands of God. Know that each day while you are living in this world you are subject to continual temptation and danger. Until the time the Lord takes us to be with Himself, never tolerate the slightest negligence in yourself or be careless and foolish. Beware of danger in the midst of your safety; beware of potholes on the smooth road; beware of entrapment during your times of feasting; beware of the sword and spear while you are having fun. People normally rest from work and sleep soundly—but the devil does not sleep! Like a roaring lion he roams around everywhere, by day and by night, seeking whom he may devour. If we are watchful and wary every moment, no harm will befall us. If we are negligent and careless, the consequences will be dreadful.

After reading how Shimei was killed because he neglected Solomon's warning, we are forewarned to be wary and watchful. After reading that even Solomon the king, the wisest man, neglected God's warning and offended God and was cursed, does not this cause us to close the book and grieve? Solomon punished Shimei, yet he himself became Shimei the second! If we do not guard ourselves with watchfulness and caution, soon we could become Shimei the third! In the future, people might read about our catastrophe and sigh for us as we sigh for Shimei and Solomon today. What a sorrowful matter that would be!

- - - - - - -

Background verses used in the above text:
[1] 1 Kings 2:36-46
[2] 1 Kings 9:1-9
[3] 1 Kings 11:1-13

廿 一個外來先知的失敗

20
An Imported Prophet Fails

Let him who thinks he stands take heed lest he fall — 1 Corinthians 10:12.

Can an honorable, faithful prophet of God suddenly go wrong? We read about such a prophet and his mission in 1 Kings 13.

In the days of King Jeroboam of Israel, God commissioned a prophet from Judah to go to Bethel with a very difficult assignment. Wicked King Jeroboam was about to burn incense before the altar of the golden calf which he had set up, and this prophet was to pronounce God's curse upon the king. It was dangerous because the king had full authority over his subjects and their property so that even the officials of the kingdom dared not provoke his anger, much less a man of God who came from a distance and had no position, authority or reputation in their territory. If King Jeroboam should want to kill him, it would be as easy as turning the palm of his hand. What this unnamed prophet was told by the Lord to do was, to human thinking, as foolish as trying to strike a rock with an egg. But because this man of God wanted to be faithful to God, he did not take account of the danger but set his face obediently to make the journey from Judah to Bethel, being determined to speak all the words God told him to speak. Such loyalty, such courage, causes all who read the account to admire him. One of our Chinese sayings is, "One looks up to a worthy man with the utmost respect; although unable to attain his stature, yet one's heart inclines toward him."

But calamity loomed! When Jeroboam heard the curse pronounced by the man of God, his anger rose like a flame and he stretched out his hand to command his guards to arrest the man of God, shouting, "Seize him!" The man of God was about to be caught; at the very least he would be flogged or sent to jail. More likely, he would be beheaded. But we don't need to worry about the man of God. God not only put this difficult and high-risk commission upon the shoulders of His servant, but according to His faithfulness and promise, God was protecting and caring for His servant. When the guards were about to lay hands on the man of God they noticed that the king's attitude had suddenly changed and his voice began to tremble. They were shocked to see that "the king's hand which he stretched out against him [had] dried up, so that he could not draw it back to himself." The king's hand had become as ugly as a hand dug out from a grave. Then the king began to plead with the man of God, "Please, entreat the Lord your God and pray for me, that my hand may be restored to me." Sizing up the situation, the guards dared not lay hands on the man of God but stood in silence to see what else would happen. They were afraid for their king. They might have been speculating that if the king's hand remained withered and outstretched, unable to bend, how would he carry out his kingly duties? How could he live normally? What a tragedy! While they were imagining the worst, they saw the man of God lift up his eyes and pray for the king. As soon as the short prayer was finished, they saw the king's withered hand immediately healed. Not only could he bend it again, but it was restored to its original texture.

How great was the power of God! How true is God's promise! In a moment a powerful king's rage could be changed to humble pleading. A man of God with nothing in his hand, and not begging for mercy before a king with great authority, could be the victorious one in such a situation. This shows that no one can fight against a God who controls heaven and earth with the highest authority. Whoever thinks he can resist God, or harm anyone who fears God, is asking for trouble.

People of God, what are you afraid of? Men in lofty positions and with authority are only human! God does not allow men to hurt one who is faithful to Him. But if God is angry with a man for disobedience, he ought to fear the wrath of God.

But this prophet's good conduct was not limited to his obedience in delivering God's message. After his prayer for Jeroboam was answered, Jeroboam invited him to his palace for a meal and offered to give him a reward. The prophet firmly excused himself, saying, "If you were to give me half your house I would not go with you, nor would I eat bread or drink water in this place. For so it was commanded me by the word of the Lord...." For a common person to be invited by any king to eat in his palace was a very honored privilege. And a gift from the king certainly would have been very precious. But this man of God, obeying and fearing God, declined both the king's invitation and gift, leaving Bethel promptly to journey back to Judah as God had instructed. This man of God not only did not fear the king's worldly power, but he also could not be tempted with greed for riches. He truly was a model prophet.

Many prophets have conveyed the word of God to men. In the beginning they may have been very true and loyal, not counting any hardship and danger too great. They spoke what God commanded and accomplished the work He committed to them. But after they accomplished their task, they naturally began to receive love and respect from men. They began to take to themselves all the enjoyment of wealth and glory. They began to be greedy and fall into the snare of the devil and no longer heeded the commandments of God. They only sought to please men. On the one hand they kept the profit and glory to themselves; on the other hand they were eager to attain still more enjoyment and fame. They became fallen prophets. This kind of prophet has a good beginning but an unfortunate end. We can see this sort of thing in the church today. Many begin well but do not remain faithful to the end. How heartbreaking this is! What the prophet had spoken came to pass not long afterward. The altar was split apart and the ashes poured out from the altar according to the prophecy which the man had received from the Lord. Moreover, his prayer on behalf of the king had been effective because he was an obedient and fearless prophet.

Today the church is in a sad state, burning incense to all kinds of "golden calves" and worshiping at strange altars. Many preachers who should be rebuking sin with God's Word have become silent. Among them, some are afraid to risk danger and calamity, and so they dare not open their mouths for God. Others are out for their own benefit, which requires that they please men. Therefore they cannot speak the truth of God. They can only beg for mercy and try to raise their support so that they may not lack food and clothing. Then they think they will be satisfied. To talk with them and remind them about being faithful to God is like "trying to skin a tiger." At this time, what the church urgently needs is prophets who are not afraid of power people, who are not afraid of any danger, who are not greedy nor seeking for vain glory but who come right out and speak for God. If there are such persons, God will greatly use them and be with them, granting spiritual authority to them so that the word spoken through them will be full of amazing power. Certainly their prayers will be answered too. God will protect them in times of danger. If people want to hurt them, God will deliver them. Not only will He not allow them to be ashamed before their enemies, He will cause their enemies to tremble before them. Such people are honored vessels in God's hand, treasured in the church and a glory in the world. The church can get along very well without rich people, or respected people, or able administrators, or good preachers, but not without this kind of prophet. Only such prophets can accomplish God's will and glorify God's name. Only such prophets are worthy to be called prophets and men of God. How many such men of God are found in the church today?

Unfortunately, when this exemplary man of God left Bethel after his great success in obedience, he had a sudden, unexpected failure. He transgressed the very commandment of God that he had quoted to the king and accepted the invitation of an old prophet to take food

An Imported Prophet Fails

and rest in that forbidden territory. It was not his own determination to sin, but he acted in response to the old prophet who had heard of him and pursued him, offering him hospitality. Though he was reluctant when first invited, and repeated the Lord's command to him which forbade him from doing so, the old prophet prevailed. The old prophet convincingly reported that God had spoken to him by an angel and that he was to tell the man from Judah to accept his invitation. The Bible says, "But he lied to him." While they were eating in the old prophet's house, the word of the Lord actually did come to the old prophet and he involuntarily cried out to the man of God, "Thus says the Lord, 'Because you have disobeyed the command of the Lord, and have not observed the commandment which the Lord your God commanded you.... your body shall not come to the grave of your fathers.' " And so it did come to pass: as the man of God from Judah had been forewarned, he was punished by God. On the way home after leaving the old prophet, he was killed on the road by a lion. This great man of God was not defeated on his way to accomplish his task, nor during his encounter with Jeroboam, but after he had victoriously left the king. The defeat was not in the presence of the wicked man worshiping the golden calf, but before a fellow prophet. What a regrettable episode! Does not this cause us to be soberly on guard?

What kind of a person was that old prophet that he would deliberately cause another prophet to transgress? He invited him to eat at his home—wasn't that just a sign of generous hospitality? Was it out of his good heart or with evil intent? And why did not God punish that lying old prophet instead of punishing the good man of God who had been deceived? The answers to these questions provide us with some important and sober insights and warnings. Every Christian should take them seriously.

Some might think that the old prophet was a false prophet. I do not believe that idea is accurate. If he had been a false prophet, the Bible would have told us plainly. This portion of Scripture calls him "old prophet" three times, and four times refers to him just as "the prophet." This old prophet was not a *false* one but a *fallen* one. He was a prophet who had lost his power and testimony, a prophet just hanging on to his life. I believe that my conclusion is based on the facts of the record and not on my own imagination.

Recall that the sinner king, Jeroboam, who set up the golden calf and its altar, was currently living in the city of Bethel and the old prophet was also a resident there. Yet the old prophet apparently kept silent, never rebuking the king nor pointing out his sin, never preaching against this great wickedness. Because of this, God had to choose and send a man of God from another place to pronounce the curse. If the old prophet had had the courage and obedience of the man of God from Judah, God would not have needed to import a servant. He could have used the old prophet who was right on the spot. Unfortunately, the old prophet was a fallen prophet.

The Bible nevertheless still refers to him as a prophet, indicating that he obviously had spoken for God and worked for God in time past. But as he grew older, he must have turned into a weak, self-indulgent person. He may have begun to care more for his own welfare and safety. He was afraid that if he went to rebuke the king the worst might happen and he could be killed by the king; or at the very least, he might be imprisoned. Or perhaps his property would be confiscated and he be sent into exile. Even if he was not directly concerned for himself, he was concerned for his family. Because he valued worldly things so highly, he gradually lost the heart to speak for God. He saw with his own eyes that the king was leading the people astray into wicked ways in the very city where he lived, and yet he kept his mouth shut. This fact certainly points up that he was a fallen prophet, having lost his power and testimony.

Let us notice further. It seems that this old prophet actually deceived the other prophet from a good heart and not from any evil intention. Some may speculate that he was jealous of the man of God from Judah and wanted him to fail. If we read this incident carefully, however, we do not find evidence to come to this conclusion. Notice that he later took the body of the man of God from the roadside where it lay beside his donkey, and brought it back to his own city. He even let him be buried in his own grave. Does not that show that he had not acted out of evil intentions? Again, consider how he charged his children: "When I die, bury me in the grave in which the man of God is buried; lay my bones beside his bones." This shows his lack of jealous motivation and expresses his sincere love for him. Because he could no longer be with his friend in life, he only hoped to be with him in the grave in death. Based on these facts, I believe we may logically conclude that when he deceived the man from Judah, it was not out of evil intent but probably from his good heart.

Some might question, "If this was the case, why then did he deceive the man of God?" This is the point we especially want to pay attention to. The old prophet seemed to be so preoccupied with his own welfare, making provision for his flesh, that the love he manifested toward the prophet from Judah was on that human level too. He probably had no intention of causing the prophet to transgress. He was probably genuinely concerned that the man of God was returning on his long journey hungry and tired. He might truly have loved that man of God and was concerned for his health. He wanted him to rest and take nourishment. He reasoned that after he had provided him a good meal, he would send him on his way to Judah. He considered rest and food as more essential than to obey the strict letter of the commandment of God so clearly given to the prophet from Judah. This reflected his carelessness toward spiritual things and his priority on ease and comfort in this life. When the man of God told him that God had forbidden him to take food and drink in Bethel, he then cunningly deceived the man of God and won him over to accept his hospitality.

When a prophet faithfully serves God, he must consider God's command as more important than his own fame, benefit, enjoyment and safety. He must put priority on fulfilling God's commands to him and completing the tasks God has given him, being willing to give up all his own benefits in the process. He is not to feel that he is at all unfortunate or deprived of all these good things. He is not to consider that he is making unusual sacrifices. He is to deal both with himself and those he loves by the same standard. After a prophet falls, he considers his own fame, benefit, enjoyment and safety to be more important than God's command and work. He would rather disobey God's command and neglect God's work than risk suffering, harm or loss to himself. Yes, the old prophet truly dealt with the man of God from a well-intentioned feeling of human love. He loved him as he loved himself, with a self-gratifying motivation. But this kind of love is the corrupted love of a fallen prophet. This kind of love is a device of Satan to harm God's people. When the Lord Jesus told His disciples that He must go to Jerusalem to be betrayed and condemned to death, Peter used this same kind of human love to misadvise his Master, urging Him not to risk such danger. But the Lord knew well that this was a scheme of Satan to prevent Him from completing God's will and God's work. So He rebuked the devil who was using Peter, saying, "Get behind Me, Satan! You are a stumbling block to Me; for you are not setting your mind on God's interests, but man's."[2] Unfortunately, that man of God from Judah did not see as clearly as Jesus saw, otherwise he would not have been deceived so easily.

Many prophets have been like that old fallen prophet. Certainly at one time they were used by God and spoke for Him. As the years went by and they got older, and as their experience also increased greatly, they should have been more useful to God and helpful to others. Unfortunately, they instead began to love the world more and make more provision for the flesh, and ended up as fallen prophets. Gradually they dared not rebuke sin any more, nor speak out against anything that was being done contrary to God's Word. Even less did they dare to offend anyone, because they were afraid of damaging their own reputation, respect, benefits and enjoyment of the things of life. They became afraid of meeting dangers and calamities. They entirely lost their power and testimony, becoming increasingly careless about the things of God. They were no longer concerned with God's commands and God's work. They loved their own flesh and made provision for it. They loved themselves and those who belonged to them. Such fallen prophets not only can no longer help people, but they mislead others. They are just like sunken ships at the bottom of a river or sea; not only are they unable to carry passengers or cargo, but they will eventually become obstacles to other ships which may strike them and sink, ending up with the same fate.

The most serious aspect that harms people is that old prophets still ride along on their former reputations. In years past they truly spoke for God and actually helped many people. They continue to be respected for what they did formerly. They never led people astray and therefore people now take for granted that what they say could

An Imported Prophet Fails

never be wrong. No one suspects that now their thoughts and ideas are quite different from before. Now the road they are taking is not the same as before. When they were true to God, what they said was certainly from God and not from men. Their former intention was to please God first. So what they used to say was a great help to people and their footsteps could be safely followed by others. But after they have fallen, what they say is from men and not from God. Now they are not putting God first. So what they say now can harm people. The direction they are going is actually down a road of rebellion against God. If believers still take heed to what they say and follow them for their former reputation's sake, they too will fall into the same sin and calamity, just as the man of God did when he was harmed by the old prophet.

The false prophet certainly does much damage; but true prophets, after they have fallen, harm people no less—even more. Yes, we should beware of false prophets. At the same time we should beware of fallen prophets. Never for a moment think that a prophet who was once faithful to God will always be faithful, nor that his words now will always be accurate just because his words helped people before. The most important thing to watch is the present manner of life of a prophet. Notice whether he compromises with sin; see if he pleases men instead of God; observe whether he regards his own well-being, property, reputation and security more than he regards God's commands. Is he afraid of God or men? Pay attention to the motivations of his heart in word and deed—are they for God or men? If he compromises with sin, tries to please man more than God, looks to his own benefits more than God's work, if he is afraid of men and not God, then you will know that he has become a fallen prophet. If you don't want to be tempted to fall into danger yourself, you should steer clear of him; otherwise, woe to you!

Another matter needs our attention. When the old prophet went after the man of God, he found him sitting under an oak tree. We can just imagine what mood the true man of God was in, sitting by the wayside on his way home. When he had first come to Bethel, he must have been excited and very much on guard lest he might suddenly weaken and become unable to do the work God had commanded him to do. When he was standing before King Jeroboam, he must have been praying without ceasing, pleading with the Lord to keep him steady and courageous so that he would not retreat or panic. When the king invited him back to the palace, he must have been alert and watchful, lest he be tempted and fail. Now, after he had left the city of Bethel victoriously, he must have been greatly relaxed and relieved, rejoicing that he had not panicked nor retreated nor failed because of greed. He must have thought that all the battles were now over, that all danger had passed. He may have rationalized that now it was not necessary for him to be that vigilant. He was very contented and at ease, sitting under the oak tree for a well-deserved little rest. Alas! At that very moment when his guard was down, when he thought he was safe, a most terrible crisis was looming for which he was unprepared. He was vulnerable. It was *after* his great victory that he fell into that disastrous failure!

Not only did *this* man of God fail under such circumstances. *Many* believers have failed in the same way—right after great successes. Many failed because of pride over their accomplishments; others, though not proud, were nevertheless negligent and careless, believing there was no danger. Such attitudes caused their downfall. Let us understand that we live a day at a time on earth and every day is a day of temptation and battle. Not one day goes by without the need to be watchful. The more we think we are safe, the more we need to be vigilant. Along life's way there are many dangers. The sly devil will attack us any time, any place, through anyone or anything, and by any means. We should have an attitude of daily watchfulness as if we were approaching the edge of a cliff or walking on thin ice. If we are not careful, the result will be inconceivable!

Notice the word spoken by the old prophet. There is one sentence that is most perilous and unquestionably harms people. "I also am a prophet like you." When the old prophet invited the man of God to dine in his home, the man perhaps was surprised to find someone in the city who feared the Lord and had not followed the wicked path of the king. For even if God had not commanded him not to eat and drink with the wicked local population, he would not have been inclined to take hospitality in such a wicked city as Bethel. He would have been justified in not trusting anyone nor listening to the words of any of the local people. But when he heard the word of assurance

An Imported Prophet Fails

by the old prophet that he also was a prophet, he was falsely assured and his attitude became relaxed. Now he knew that there was a prophet there, and since he was a prophet, he would certainly not be harmed by him. He took for granted that the old prophet would speak and act according to God's commands. He concluded that to have fellowship with such a person would be safe enough and he would not need to be on his guard. Never would he have dreamed that this generous and hospitable man was a fallen prophet.

There are many Christians destroyed under similar circumstances today. When they are in contact with non-believers and do business with them, it is with an attitude of watchfulness. They know they dare not trust them or take their words at face value; much less do they dare to follow them in doing what is not pleasing to God. But when they meet a professing Christian, they slacken their vigilance. Who would guess that that Christian might be a fallen Christian or even a false one? When they were among the non-Christians, because of their watchfulness they did not fall or commit sin. But when they were with fellow Christians, they fell and committed sin. We often hear of and see such cases.

There was a certain person who believed in the Lord after having been a lifelong gambler. When he became a Christian, he entirely abandoned the gambling habit. Although many friends and relatives enticed him and tried to force him to gamble again, he would firmly refuse. Five years after his conversion, never having touched any gambling devices, he was invited one day to a wedding at the home of a relative. After the wedding and feast, the people set up a table to play *mah-jong* [a well-known Chinese gambling game]. He was asked to join them. He answered, "I don't play because I am a Christian." A person came over to him and said, "Mr. X, are you a Christian? I also am a Christian like you. I believed in the Lord more than ten years ago. But I never stopped playing *mah-jong*. *Mah-jong* is not like stealing. It is not a sin to play only occasionally. How do you think you can win people to the Lord if you have interests that are too different from theirs?" As soon as he heard, "I also am a Christian like you," his attitude became relaxed. He concluded that he did not need to be so watchful any more. He felt that he had now met a companion walking in the heavenly way. When he realized that the other man was his senior in the faith, he formed a good impression of him, respecting him as one who had gone before him into the kingdom. He judged that this man must surely have a more mature spiritual attitude than his own. He entirely cast off his anxiety and vigilance and was willing to accept his elder brother's suggestion. How easily he was persuaded that the strict stand that he had been taking toward gambling was actualy not necessary! From that time on he began to return to his old bad habit. Scores of unbelieving relatives through all those five long years had not been able to shake his determination not to gamble because he was a Christian. But a self-styled "Christian," lightly speaking only a few words, had caused him to gamble again after he had resolved never to do so. What a heartbreaking episode!

Many Christians fail not because of the influence of godless people but because of the influence of bad Christians. Many believers who worked for God have failed, not by being tempted by those who did not know God, but by the failure of fallen preachers. "I also am a Christian like you." "I also am God's worker like you." This saying has done damage to so many believers who were not watchful. We should be especially vigilant if we meet someone whom we don't know well who claims, "I also am a Christian like you," or "I also am God's servant like you." Never take at face value what they say, because you don't know if they are true or false, presently walking with God or fallen. The man of God from Judah was greatly harmed because he believed the old prophet too quickly. Are you going to fall into the same pit?

One might ask: "The man of God from Judah who was deceived by that old prophet was not the one at fault. Why then did God punish him?" But I ask you, did he truly have no fault? On what do you base that? When he was commissioned to go to Bethel, wasn't God clear enough to command him not to eat or drink there until he returned? When God has firmly spoken, how can it be changed? God is not changeable like "something ordered at dawn, changed at eve." Since God commanded him not to eat or drink in Bethel, He would not suddenly reverse His command. When he heard the old prophet say that an angel brought the word of God, he should have questioned those words. At least he should have directly asked

God, "God, didn't You bid me not to eat and drink in Bethel before I came here? Did you really ask this old prophet to look for me and invite me to his home to eat and drink now?" If he had inquired of God in this way, he would never have been deceived by the old prophet. Maybe God would somehow have revealed that He had *not* spoken to the old prophet to invite him, or maybe God would have just been silent. Either way, the man would have been suspicious that the old prophet was lying. Too bad he believed the old prophet so quickly, without even testing his story or inquiring of God. He rashly took the statement at face value from one he had just met. Do you still maintain that he was not guilty?

One thing more—the will of God cannot suddenly be *yes*, then *no*. If a thing is right, it will be right forever. If a thing is wrong, it will always be wrong. God's word is truth. When the Lord Jesus prayed, He said to God, "Sanctify them in the truth; Thy word is truth."[3] Truth will never change, therefore the word of God never changes. "Forever, O Lord, Thy word is settled in heaven."[4] Paul also explained this in his epistle: "Therefore, I was not vacillating when I intended to do this, was I?...that with me there should be yes, yes and no, no at the same time? But as God is faithful, our word to you is not yes and no.... For as many as may be the promises of God, in Him they are yes; wherefore also by Him is our Amen to the glory of God through us."[5] If there is one thing we have already understood to be God's will, we should never question it, no matter what other people say; especially, let us not accept anything contrary to what God has already spoken. If there are things we are not sure of, naturally we should consider some suggestions and counsel from others. Then we should ask God to show us which advice conforms to His will. If we are very sure already and know from Him that a certain thing is God's will for us to do or not to do, then we should never disobey that command and seek for a second opinion.

The man of God from Judah accepted the invitation of the old prophet when he was tired and hungry and needed some nourishment to strengthen him. He had come a long way to Bethel, had pronounced the curse to Jeroboam, had left the city gate, and was returning home by a different route, all without food and water to sustain him. How intensely hungry and thirsty he must have been at that time!

It was right at that weak moment the old prophet deceived him. If he had not been so physically depleted, he might have considered more carefully and asked God about it. Under such trying circumstances he gave in to the flesh. When believers have some special need, that is the time the devil moves in and attacks them most severely. They may be poor or hungry, be despised or disliked, intimidated, threatened, oppressed or attacked. Under those circumstances they sorely need money or food, defense, comfort, sympathy, help, love, understanding or advice. It is at those critical times that the devil will use "old prophets" to tempt them, offering them schemes and leading them astray. The words of fallen prophets clearly do damage to believers. Because they think such a man is harmless and that he is offering just exactly what they need, it becomes very easy to listen to what he says and accept what he offers. But know this, it is a clever strategy of Satan. We should be especially watchful if we have some extreme need. Make no provision for the flesh! Don't use man's method to appease hunger, poverty, to satisfy a fleshly desire or to avoid persecution or adversity. Rather, go ahead and suffer according to God's will and never disobey God's command in order to avoid danger.

Some might still ask: "The man of God was deceived, but the old prophet was the deceiver. The deceived one was duly punished, but the deceiver got off with no punishment. How can God be so unfair?" The way I see it is that what God did was *very* fair. The man of God from Judah was faithful to God, was pleasing to God, so God dealt with him with exceptional strictness. As the Scripture says, "Blessed is the man whom Thou dost chasten, O Lord, and dost teach out of Thy law"[6]; and also, "My son, do not reject the discipline of the Lord, or loathe His reproof, for whom the Lord loves He reproves, even as a father the son in whom he delights.''[7] Yes, this man of God was killed by a lion. It was God's punishment because he really did disobey God's command. But in the day of resurrection, he will still receive the full reward given to a faithful prophet. His faithfulness in being fearless toward authority, not seeking wealth, giving no thought to his personal safety and enjoyment, will not be overlooked or uncompensated by the Lord. As to the fallen prophet, he was already useless before God, worthless; though he remained

An Imported Prophet Fails

alive, yet he was as if dead. It was not worth it for God to correct and punish him, so God just let him alone.

Again some might question: "Since this old prophet was fallen and useless, how was it that God still spoke through him?" Yes, God did speak once more through him. He prophesied what would happen to the man of God from Judah for his disobedience. God raises up prophets as His spokesmen to rebuke the wicked for their sins, warning them how to escape the wrath of God. He asks them to convey His promise of mercy. He lets people know that if they obey God, they will receive blessing. Because this old prophet, still hanging on to his life, had departed from his commission, God could no longer use him to do those major things. The only thing he could do after the old prophet had been such a deceiver was to let him pronounce the punishment that he, himself, had brought on the man of God. At the same time his own sentence was also pronounced, because he was the one who had tempted and deceived him. When the word of God came to him on that occasion, actually it was not that God was using him again, but that God was punishing him; not respecting him, but actually disgracing him.

We can imagine that from the time the old prophet heard that the man of God had been torn to death by the lion on the roadside until the day he himself died, he must have felt extremely guilty and remorseful. What anguish he must have had in his heart! He probably wept bitterly whenever he thought of the death of that true man of God he had caused. He must have been deeply remorseful because he could no longer be used as God's instrument and because the man of God who really *could* speak for God was killed because of the way he had deceived him. He must have suffered under this realization for the rest of his life. His carnal love damaged others and also harmed himself, causing him to undergo anguish, bitterness and sorrow until he died. We should never accept the carnal love offered by others; nor should we love others with this fleshly, human kind of love. Not only does this kind of love profit nothing to anyone, but on the contrary, it injures others as well as ourselves. There is a saying, "A gentleman loves people with virtue; a despicable man loves people conditionally." Believers should love people with the kind of love expressed in the Word of God. Only this kind of love is genuine love.

This love will benefit people, never exploit people. Apart from the will of God, all other love should be abstained from by Christians. After so thoroughly studying this episode for our own exhortation, we cannot help but feel sorry for the man of God from Judah; we can't stop sighing with pity for that old fallen prophet. But it is more important for each of us to be ever watchful, trembling with fear at this warning for ourselves. May God protect us through this example so that we might not follow the disastrous road which these two took. Otherwise, after we have felt sorrow and sighing for *them*, others will feel the same about *us!*

- - - - - - -

Background verses used in the above text:
[1] Entire episode taken from 1 Kings 13:1-32
[2] Matthew 16:23
[3] John 17:17
[4] Psalm 119:89
[5] 2 Corinthians 1:17-20
[6] Psalm 94:12
[7] Proverbs 3:11,12